GO TILL YOU GUESS
BIBLE GAMES

A Bible Recreation Book of Bible Facts,
Scenes, Persons, and Places

BY

AMOS R. WELLS

LONDON
PICKERING & INGLIS LTD

PICKERING & INGLIS LTD
29 LUDGATE HILL, LONDON EC4M 7BP
26 BOTHWELL STREET, GLASGOW G2 6PA

Copyrighted, 1930, by
Baker Book House Company

ISBN 0 7208 0313 6

Cat. No. 01//0710

First printing 1970
Second printing 1973
This British edition 1974

This edition is issued by
special arrangements with
BAKER BOOK HOUSE
the American publishers

Printed in Great Britain by
Lowe & Brydone (Printers) Ltd, Thetford, Norfolk

HOW TO USE THIS BOOK

Did you ever play the old-fashioned game of "Throwing Light"?
It's like this.

The leader remarks, "I'm thinking of a mighty hunter."

"Nimrod!" immediately shouts a cock-sure person. "Leatherstocking!" "Daniel Boone!" say others.

The leader shakes his head and calmly proceeds. "He is dead now. He was a writer, and he was descended from a Georgia family."

"Frank L. Stanton!" comes a hasty interruption, but the leader goes on.

"Stanton wasn't a hunter, so far as I know. This man was of Dutch descent. He was in very poor health when a boy, but became very strong through exercise."

"Robert Louis Stevenson," timidly remarks some one without much thought. The leader disregards him and continues.

"He lived in New York City and became a well-known traveller and explorer."

"Henry M. Stanley!" a confident voice pipes up.

The leader says, "Not so bad, but Stanley fails to fit in several points. The man I am thinking of had poor eyes and remarkably good teeth. He graduated from Harvard. He lived on a ranch." Here the leader begins to speak fast. "He was a civil service reformer. He was a police commissioner. He was a soldier. He was Assistant Secretary of the Navy. He was governor. He was Vice-President. He was President. He flourished 'the big stick.' He——." But probably long before the leader reaches this point the entire party has shouted, "*Theodore Roosevelt!*"

Then the leader designates another person to think of some one or some thing and "throw light" in his turn.

This is a book of "throwing light" on the Bible. Each little section of the book deals with a separate Bible character or event or geographical feature or tree or animal or object or famous sentence or something of the sort. And each section tells about its subject, item after item, and the reader is to take for his motto, "Go till you guess!"

If he guesses the person or thing with line one, his score for that section is 1; if he has to go on to the second line before he guesses, his score is 2;

he may not guess it until he reaches the very last line, when his score will be 5 or 6, or whatever the number of that line is. If he does not guess it at all, his score is 10. It will be seen that the victor will be the one with the lowest score, and the best record that can be made will consist all of ones; that is, for twenty sections the best possible record would be 20.

In " throwing light " the facts least likely to furnish a clue are placed first, of course, and those that are quite certain to " give the thing away " are reserved for the last; therefore only those well informed regarding the Bible will make a record consisting of ones and twos and threes.

For the use of those that want to trace all these facts, many Bible references are given with the answers in the back of the book. Reading these references will make the book exceedingly instructive.

Except as noted, the American Standard Version of the Bible is used throughout, by permission of the owners of the copyright, the International Council of Religious Education.

The entire Bible is covered by " Go Till You Guess," and familiarity with these recreations will give you a good working knowledge of Holy Writ.

This book is for both solitary and social use. It will serve to fill with pleasure and profit many an otherwise lonely hour. When a company is brought together, one may produce the book and begin to " throw light," bidding his hearers to " go till they guess." He must make sure at the start that they understand that his string of successive bits of information all relates to the same subject, and they will at once catch the idea. There are enough very easy sections in the book to lure any company on for a long time, while there are enough hard sections to make the book interesting even to experienced Bible students.

You may use the book at home, and especially for Sunday afternoons or for home gatherings of any kind. It may be used for church socials and the socials of young people's societies and Sunday-school classes. It is entirely different from the author's previous book, " Know Your Bible? " and the two volumes supplement each other admirably. Whoever enjoys one of them will be sure to enjoy the other.

Now let the hunt begin, and *Go Till You Guess!*

AMOS R. WELLS

Auburndale, Mass.

Go Till You Guess

SERIES I

Bible Books

[Read each description a line at a time, and *Go Till You Guess*. Your score for each item is the number of the line at which you obtained the answer, and the lowest total wins.]

No. 1.

1. This Book has been called " The Gospel of Common Sense."
2. It is an appeal for practical Christianity.
3. It urges that " faith, if it have not works, is dead."
4. It contains a wonderful chapter on the power of the tongue.
5. It was written by one of our Lord's brothers.

No. 2.

1. This Book is a marvellously comprehensive and powerful study of human life.
2. It closes with a fine statement of " the whole duty of man."
3. Its refrain is: " Vanity of vanities, all is vanity."
4. It declares: " Cast thy bread upon the waters; for thou shalt find it after many days."
5. It tells us that " a living dog is better than a dead lion."

No. 3.

1. This Book is a series of accounts of great Hebrew patriots and warriors.
2. They extend from the times of Joshua to the times of Samuel.

3. There were thirteen of these saviors of the people.
4. One of them was a king.
5. The greatest of them was Gideon.

No. 4.

1. This has been called " The Gospel of Spiritual Insight."
2. It is the greatest book ever written.
3. It was written by " the beloved disciple."
4. It contains the account of the raising of Lazarus.
5. It reports Christ's discourse and prayer at the last supper.

No. 5.

1. There is no mention of God in this Book.
2. It is, however, an account of a wonderful divine providence.
3. It presents vivid pictures of two queens.
4. The villain of the Book is hanged.
5. Its most famous sentence is probably this: " Who knoweth whether thou art not come to the kingdom for such a time as this? "

No. 6.

1. The name of this Book means " The Second Law."
2. The Book consists of an address in three installments.
3. It is a Book which closed a great era and prepared for another.
4. It contains " the blessings and the cursings."
5. It contains: " Thou shalt love Jehovah thy God with all thy heart, and with all thy soul, and with all thy might."

No. 7.

1. This is the only anonymous Book of the New Testament.
2. It has been attributed to many, including Paul, Barnabas, and Apollos.

3. It contains the famous Hero Chapter.

4. It contains the statement that Christ was " in all points tempted like as we are, yet without sin."

5. It contains the statement that " Jesus Christ is the same yesterday and to-day, yea and forever."

No. 8.

1. This is the great missionary Book of the Old Testament.

2. It pictures a famous runaway from duty.

3. It tells about the conversion of a great heathen city.

4. It is a presentation of God's mercy.

5. One of its sentences is, " All thy waves and thy billows passed over me."

No. 9.

1. This is the great missionary Book of the New Testament.

2. It was written by a doctor.

3. It describes three unequalled missionary journeys.

4. It contains an account of a sermon which won three thousand souls.

5. It pictures the work of the greatest foreign missionary.

No. 10.

1. This is a Book full of wonderful little sentences.

2. It contains the finest of all descriptions of wisdom.

3. It contains a powerful account of a drunkard.

4. In it is a beautiful portrait of a virtuous woman.

5. A sample sentence is: " The wicked flee when no man pursueth; but the righteous are bold as a lion."

No. 11.

1. This is the Book of Beginnings.

2. It presents a marvellous summary of the most ancient history.

3. It also gives four extended biographies of remarkable interest and value.

4. In this Book, too, are many subordinate portraits that are full of distinctive vitality.

5. The Book includes a story which a company of Boston authors once voted to be the most perfect story ever written.

No. 12.

1. This is a glorious little Book, by Paul, of only one chapter.
2. It is about a man named " Profitable."
3. It was written to one of Paul's friends in Asia Minor.
4. The purpose of the writing is to urge forgiveness.
5. In it the writer speaks of himself as " Paul the aged."

SERIES II

Bible Rivers and Other Waters

[Read each description a line at a time, and *Go Till You Guess*. Your score for each item is the number of the line at which you obtained the answer, and the lowest total wins.]

No. 1.

1. This river flows into the Jordan from the east.
2. It cuts Mount Gilead in two.
3. It made the western boundary of the Ammonites.
4. Jacob crossed this river when he returned from Mesopotamia with his family.
5. Near this river Jacob wrestled with the angel.

No. 2.

1. This river, on account of its great fall, is called " the descender."
2. It is 104 miles long.
3. Its source is 1,000 feet above the level of the Mediterranean and its mouth 1,292 below that level.
4. Twice the river was miraculously crossed.
5. Once a miraculous cure was worked by its waters.
6. It is by far the most important river of Palestine.

No. 3.

1. The name of this many-curved river signifies " tortuous."
2. The soldiers of Sisera were swept away by the current of this river.
3. The priests of Baal, defeated by Elijah, were slain on the bank of this river.
4. It is called " that ancient river."
5. It is perhaps the second river of Palestine in importance.
6. It flows through the Plain of Esdraelon and empties into the Mediterranean.

No. 4.

1. The name of this pool means " house of mercy."
2. Its waters were supposed to have healing qualities.
3. Five large porches surrounded the pool.
4. It was situated near the sheep gate, in northeastern Jerusalem.
5. An angel was said to come to this pool and agitate the water.
6. Our Lord worked one of his miracles at this pool.

No. 5.

1. The original name of this sea was Chinnereth.
2. Three other names are given it in the Bible.

3. It is nearly thirteen miles long and its greatest width is seven and a half miles.

4. Its surface lies 682.5 feet below the level of the Mediterranean.

5. It is subject to sudden and severe storms.

6. On this sea Christ worked some of his most wonderful miracles.

No. 6.

1. This is a pool, whose name means " sent," referring to the sending of water through an aqueduct.

2. It receives, through an aqueduct, the water of the Fountain of the Virgin.

3. Near by was a tower which fell, killing eighteen persons.

4. The pool is fifty-eight feet long, eighteen broad, and nineteen deep.

5. It is situated at the southeastern corner of Jerusalem.

6. Christ once sent a blind man to wash in this pool.

No. 7.

1. This is a sea sometimes called the Sea of the Arabah or Plain.

2. Its surface is 1,292 feet lower than the ocean level.

3. It is about 47 miles long and 9½ miles broad.

4. It is 1,300 feet deep at its deepest.

5. Its water contains about four times as much salt as ocean water.

6. Its common name is derived from the supposed (but not complete) absence of life in its waters.

No. 8.

1. This river is formed by two others called the White and the Blue.

2. For more than 1,800 miles it traverses two Bible countries.

3. Its annual floods raise its height by from twenty-three to forty feet.

4. If there is no flood a famine results.
5. The river was associated with the life of Joseph.
6. It was associated dramatically with the career of Moses.

No. 9.

1. This is called in the Bible "the Great River" or merely "the River."
2. It was one of the rivers of Paradise.
3. It is about 1,800 miles long.
4. It was once turned into an immense excavation in order to give access to a great city.
5. It was considered the eastern boundary of the Roman Empire.
6. Abraham was born on its banks.

No. 10.

1. This body of water is often called in the Bible simply "the sea."
2. It is also called "the sea of the Philistines."
3. Sometimes it is called "the great sea."
4. Jonah sailed upon it once.
5. Paul sailed upon it many times.
6. It is two thousand miles long.

No. 11.

1. The Hebrews called this "the sea of sedge."
2. Its Greek (and modern) name is derived from the reddish-brown cliffs and hills which border it.
3. Its northern end extends into two gulfs.
4. Between these two gulfs took place the most momentous event of the Old Testament.
5. The western gulf witnessed one of the greatest of Old Testament miracles.
6. This region is closely associated with Moses.

SERIES III

Bible Speeches

[Read each description a line at a time, and *Go Till You Guess*. Your score for each item is the number of the line at which you obtained the answer, and the lowest total wins.]

No. 1.

1. This speech says that in God " we live, and move, and have our being."
2. It declares that God " made of one every nation of men."
3. The speech was made on a famous hill.
4. It was made in one of the world's most famous cities.
5. It was made by the greatest man of the New Testament.

No. 2.

1. A farewell address by the second greatest man of the Old Testament.
2. In it he says: " Here I am: witness against me before Jehovah."
3. In it he asks: " Whom have I defrauded? Whom have I oppressed? "
4. In it he says: " Far be it from me that I should sin against Jehovah in ceasing to pray for you."
5. This speech was confirmed by a thunderstorm in wheat harvest.

No. 3.

1. This address was a summary of Old Testament history.
2. It was delivered at a trial for life or death.
3. The speaker addressed his auditors as " Ye stiff-necked and uncircumcised in heart and ears."

4. The address closed with a vision of Christ.
5. The verdict was death by stoning.

No. 4.

1. Two farewell addresses by the same man, one delivered at Shechem.
2. A sentence from them: " This day I am going the way of all the earth."
3. Another sentence: " Take good heed therefore unto yourselves, that ye love Jehovah your God."
4. Another: " Choose you this day whom ye will serve."
5. The result was a solemn covenant between God and the people.

No. 5.

1. This address was made from a stairway.
2. It was made to a mob.
3. In it the speaker said: " I persecuted this Way unto the death."
4. The speech ended: " I will send thee forth far hence unto the Gentiles."
5. The result was an enraged uproar.

No. 6.

1. This speech occupies three chapters of Matthew.
2. A shorter form is given by Luke.
3. It contains the Lord's prayer.
4. It opens with eight " blesseds."
5. It closes with the parable of two foundations.

No. 7.

1. The direct results of this sermon were the greatest recorded in history.

2. In it the speaker said: " This Jesus did God raise up, whereof we all are witnesses."

3. He also said: " To you is the promise, and to your children, and to all that are afar off."

4. The speech followed one of the most wonderful events of history.

5. The speaker was the leader of the Twelve.

No. 8.

1. This address was made before a king by a prisoner.

2. In it the speaker asked: " Why is it judged incredible with you, if God doth raise the dead? "

3. He also said: " I was not disobedient unto the heavenly vision."

4. The king said: " With but little persuasion thou wouldest make me a Christian."

5. The address was made in Cæsarea.

No. 9.

1. These addresses occupy the greater part of one of the longest Books of the Bible.

2. They contain a remarkable series of blessings and curses.

3. They contain a form of the Ten Commandments.

4. They contain a summary of the Law.

5. Verses from them are placed in the phylacteries.

No. 10.

1. This address occupies three chapters of John's Gospel.

2. It contains the words, " I am the way, and the truth, and the life."

3. Also the sentence, " Ye are my friends, if ye do the things which I command you."

4. Also the promise: " If ye shall ask anything of the Father, he will give it you in my name."

5. The address was spoken in an upper room in Jerusalem.

SERIES IV

Bible Mothers

[Read each description a line at a time, and *Go Till You Guess*. Your score for each item is the number of the line at which you obtained the answer, and the lowest total wins.]

No. 1.

1. This mother, though a foreigner and a heathen, came to Jesus.
2. She begged him to heal her daughter.
3. To test her, he seemed to refuse.
4. She won him by an amazingly beautiful reply.
5. He bestowed on her pre-eminent praise.

No. 2.

1. She was the chief of all mothers that ever lived.
2. At the same time she was the saddest of all mothers.
3. She had the most wonderful of all sons.
4. She pondered his words and acts, but did not seem to understand him.
5. At his death he put her in the charge of his dearest friend.

No. 3.

1. She was the first mother.
2. She lived in western Asia.
3. She had three sons whose names we know.
4. Her oldest son slew the second son.
5. The first sin is laid to her account.

No. 4.

1. This mother, because she was childless, was tormented by a second wife, who had children.

2.   Her husband asked, " Am I not better to thee than ten sons? "

3.   As her lips moved in prayer, the priest mistook her for a drunken woman.

4.   She received a son in answer to prayer.

5.   She made him a special robe every year.

No. 5.

1.   The mother of Paul's beloved young helper.

2.   She is described as a woman of " unfeigned faith."

3.   She taught her son the Scriptures from his earliest years.

4.   He became pastor of the important church of Ephesus.

5.   Paul wrote him two wonderful letters.

No. 6.

1.   She was the mother of a man whose birth was foretold in the last two verses of the Old Testament.

2.   She became old but was childless.

3.   An angel foretold that she should bear a son.

4.   Before the son was born, she had a visit from a kinswoman from the north.

5.   The son became a great preacher, who suffered a martyr's death.

No. 7.

1.   With her and for her the greatest of the Hebrew kings committed two of the greatest crimes.

2.   The king was severely rebuked by a prophet.

3.   As was foretold, the child of this evil marriage died.

4.   Then she had a second child, who became a great king and a very wise man.

5.   But it was only through her efforts, and the prophet's, that her son became king.

No. 8.

1. This was " a great woman," who had no son.
2. She made a little room on the wall, which she set apart for a prophet.
3. In return the prophet foretold that she should have a son..
4. When the boy grew up he fell sick and died.
5. She sent for the prophet, who restored the boy to life.

No. 9.

1. This mother appeared before Solomon, claiming a babe.
2. Another woman also laid claim to it, saying that the first woman stole it from her.
3. Solomon called for a sword, and announced that he would give half of the babe to each woman.
4. The true mother was determined by her reaction to this threat.

No. 10.

1. The mother of the wife of an apostle.
2. She lived in Capernaum.
3. She was seized with a severe fever.
4. A great healer touched her hand and the fever left her.
5. At once she rose and, as was evidently her custom, ministered to the physical needs of the company.

No. 11.

1. The mother of two fishers who became apostles.
2. She joined with them in a very ambitious request.
3. She was one of those who went to the tomb on Easter morning.
4. One of her sons was the first apostle to become a martyr.
5. The other probably outlived all the apostles.

No. 12.

1.   She probably furnished the upper room for the Lord's supper.

2.   That room became a meeting place of the disciples after the resurrection.

3.   At her house the Christians met to pray for Peter's release from prison.

4.   Her son became a helper of Paul, then of Barnabas, then of Peter.

5.   He wrote one of the Gospels.

No. 13.

1.   She was the wife of the greatest of the patriarchs.

2.   Her husband twice told a half-lie about her.

3.   She reached old age without having a child.

4.   Through supernatural intervention, a son was granted her.

5.   Her husband was about to sacrifice this son, but was supernaturally prevented.

SERIES V

Bible Birds

[Read each description a line at a time, and *Go Till You Guess*. Your score for each item is the number of the line at which you obtained the answer, and the lowest total wins.]

No. 1.

1.   Christ refers to this bird as harmless.

2.   It was used as a sacrifice.

3.   It is a symbol of the Holy Spirit.

4.   It was bought and sold in the temple courts.

5.   It proved useful at the time of the flood.

No. 2.

1. The psalmist said that his youth was renewed like that of this bird.

2. Isaiah said that those that wait on the Lord shall " mount up with wings " as this bird.

3. One of the proverbs speaks of riches as flying away like this bird.

4. The Lord reminded the Israelites how he had borne them on wings, as this bird does with its young.

5. Christ said that wherever the carcass is, there these birds will be gathered.

No. 3.

1. This bird, sent from the ark, did not return.

2. The psalmist pictures Jehovah as giving food to these birds when young and clamorous.

3. The Lord, speaking to Job, asks who provides prey for this bird when its young are crying.

4. Christ bade all anxious persons to consider this bird, how God cares for it.

5. These birds fed Elijah by the brook Cherith.

No. 4.

1. The third watch of the night was marked by the call of the male of this bird.

2. This same call served as a warning to an apostle.

3. Christ compared his love for Jerusalem to the care of the female of this bird for her young.

No. 5.

1. A carrion-eating bird, which, with the kite, was not to be eaten.

2. Job speaks of a path which even the sharp eye of this bird has not seen.

3. Isaiah prophesies that Edom shall be a place for the gathering of these birds of prey.

No. 6.

1. The psalmist in his sorrow said that he had become like this bird, alone and grieving on the housetop.

2. He also speaks of this bird as nesting on the temple altars.

3. Christ speaks of God's care for these birds, though two of them are sold for a penny.

No. 7.

1. The psalmist speaks of this bird as nesting in fir-trees.

2. In one of his visions Zechariah saw two women with wings like those of this bird.

3. Jeremiah speaks of this bird as knowing the time for its migrations.

No. 8.

1. In one of the psalms of thanksgiving the people are reminded that God once sent these birds to them, together with " the bread of heaven."

2. The reference is to the supply of food given to the Israelites in the wilderness.

3. At Kibroth-hattaavah an immense supply of these birds resulted in a plague.

No. 9.

1. The Lamentations speaks of the cruelty of these birds.

2. Job speaks of being a companion to this bird.

3. The Lord, speaking to Job, bids him notice the proud waving of this bird's wings.

4. Describing the coming desolation of Babylon, Isaiah says that this bird shall dwell there.

5. Foretelling the doom of Edom, this same prophet says that it shall be a " court for " these birds.

No. 10.

1.   The psalmist speaks of this bird as having found a nest for herself in God's altar.

2.   One of the proverbs says that, like this bird in its flying, " so the curse that is causeless alighteth not."

3.   Hezekiah, in his poem describing his sickness, says that he chattered like one of these birds.

4.   Jeremiah speaks of this bird as knowing the time for its migration.

SERIES VI

Bible Parables

[Read each description a line at a time, and *Go Till You Guess*. Your score for each item is the number of the line at which you obtained the answer, and the lowest total wins.]

No. 1.

1.   This is probably to be regarded as Christ's greatest parable, " the pearl of all parables."

2.   The parable is in two parts.

3.   It was spoken for the sake of the second part, but to-day that portion is used very little as compared with the first portion.

4.   This is the parable that speaks of " a far country."

5.   This is the parable that refers to " the fatted calf."

No. 2.

1.   This is probably the best-known of the Old Testament parables.

2.   It was spoken to carry conviction to a great sinner.

3.   It was spoken by a distinguished prophet in the days of the united kingdom.

4. It was spoken to rebuke murder and adultery.
5. It was a parable about a lamb.

No. 3.

1. Christ spoke this parable in order to define a common word.
2. The parable places one man in sharp contrast to two others.
3. The scene of the parable is a cave-bordered road.
4. The parable originated a common name for a charitable person.
5. The parable ends with " Go, and do thou likewise."

No. 4.

1. This parable was spoken after the killing by one man of his seventy brothers.
2. It was spoken by one brother who escaped.
3. It was shouted from the top of a mountain.
4. The parable concerned certain trees.
5. It was spoken in the days of the Judges.

No. 5.

1. The first spoken of Christ's parables.
2. It is a parable in four parts.
3. It is a parable of heedful hearing.
4. It is an agricultural parable.
5. One of its often-used phrases is " fell by the wayside."

No. 6.

1. This parable ended the greatest of all sermons.
2. It is a parable of contrasted buildings.
3. The parable teaches obedience.
4. It introduces Palestine's dry river beds and winter torrents.
5. The closing words are often quoted, " Great was the fall thereof."

No. 7.

1. The parable of a wonderful stream.
2. The stream freshened a salt sea.
3. It was bordered by monthly-bearing fruit trees.
4. It grew rapidly deeper.
5. It issued from the temple.
6. It was a picture of the progress of true religion.

No. 8.

1. These are two similar parables about money.
2. The money in one parable is much greater than in the other.
3. One sum is represented as buried in the ground, the other as being wrapped in a napkin.
4. In common speech the two are often confused.
5. One of these parables gives us a common word signifying special ability.

No. 9.

1. A parable by the greatest Hebrew prophet.
2. A parable urging spiritual fruitfulness.
3. The parable describes an Oriental vineyard.
4. The parable pictures a vineyard bearing wild grapes.
5. It foretells the desolation of God's people and land.

No. 10.

1. This is a famous parable of prayer.
2. It contrasts pride and humility, hypocrisy and sincerity.
3. The scene of the parable is the temple.
4. The hero of the parable is a member of a despised class.
5. The parable contains the words, " God, be thou merciful to me a sinner."

No. 11.

1.　This parable was spoken by an unnamed prophet of the time of King Ahab.

2.　The prophet, on a second attempt, got himself wounded.

3.　The parable was for the rebuke of the king in the matter of Ben-hadad.

4.　It contains the sentence, " As thy servant was busy here and there, he was gone."

5.　The parable closed with a prophecy of the destruction of Ahab and his kingdom.

No. 12.

1.　The scene of this parable of Christ's is this earth, heaven, and hell.

2.　It involves a poor man, a rich man.

3.　Also it introduces certain dogs.

4.　A great patriarch comes into the parable.

5.　It contains the words, " a great gulf fixed."

SERIES VII

A Company of Kings

[Read each description a line at a time, and *Go Till You Guess*. Your score for each item is the number of the line at which you obtained the answer, and the lowest total wins.]

No. 1.

1.　The king who hardened his heart.

2.　He received more powerful warnings than any other king of history.

3. His warnings affected him nationally, religiously, and personally, but still he hardened his heart.

4. He hardened his heart so long that at last, it is said, God hardened his heart.

5. Even after he finally submitted, he tried to take back his submission.

No. 2.

1. The king before whom Paul made his famous plea.

2. Paul was then a prisoner in Cæsarea.

3. In the company was also the Roman governor of Judæa.

4. Listening to Paul also was the king's sister, a notorious woman.

5. The king was the great-grandson of another king, who was called " the Great."

No. 3.

1. The king whose acts drew from Isaiah the prophecy of Immanuel.

2. He made his son to pass through the fire.

3. He was besieged by Syria and Israel.

4. With the treasures of his palace and the temple he bought the aid of Assyria.

5. He was a king of Judah.

No. 4.

1. The king whose pride cost him more than half of his kingdom.

2. The foolish son of a very wise father.

3. The king who boasted that his little finger was thicker than his father's loins.

4. His palace and the temple were plundered by an Egyptian army.

5. He was the first sovereign of the Southern Kingdom.

No. 5.

1. The king who slew James the brother of John.

2. The king who imprisoned Peter.
3. He was the grandson of a king called " the Great."
4. He had a son of his own name who also became a king.
5. He died a horrible death, being eaten up of worms.

No. 6.

1. The good son and successor of a good king of Judah.
2. He made the great mistake of marrying his son to an idolatress.
3. He fought a battle in the garments of another king.
4. He was rebuked by the prophets for fraternizing with evil kings.
5. He sent teachers of the law of God all over his kingdom.

No. 7.

1. This king was taller than all his people by head and shoulders.
2. He was first king of his nation.
3.. He made a search for a drove of asses.
4. He consulted a witch.
5. He committed suicide.

No. 8.

1. He was king of Tyre.
2. He was a friend and helper of two great kings.
3. He helped build the first temple.
4. He contributed wood and gold.
5. He refused twenty towns in payment.

No. 9.

1. He was the first king who destroyed Jerusalem.
2. For some time before this destruction Judah was tributary to him.
3. He built great hanging gardens in his capital.
4. He carried several great companies of the Jews to his own land.
5. His pride was punished with insanity.

SERIES VIII

Bible Mountains and Hills

[Read each description a line at a time, and *Go Till You Guess*. Your score for each item is the number of the line at which you obtained the answer, and the lowest total wins.]

No. 1.

1. This mountain is within six miles of Nazareth.
2. It has been held, probably erroneously, to be the scene of the transfiguration.
3. It has a flat top.
4. It is 1,843 feet high.
5. Troops from Issachar and Zebulun met here before fighting Sisera.

No. 2.

1. The name of this mountain means " a garden."
2. On the top took place one of the most remarkable of Bible conflicts.
3. It consists of a range of hills about fifteen miles long, ending in a promontory.
4. From this mountain Elisha was summoned to raise from the dead the Shunammite's son.
5. It is situated southwest of the plain of Esdraelon.

No. 3.

1. The hill on which Abraham prepared to sacrifice Isaac.
2. The Samaritans hold, probably erroneously, that the place was near Shechem.

3. The hill in Jerusalem on which was the threshing floor of Ornan the Jebusite.

4. Solomon built his temple on this hill.

5. It is situated in eastern Jerusalem, west of the Kidron valley.

No. 4.

1. On this mountain Saul and Jonathan died.

2. Here the Philistines won a victory over the Israelites.

3. The mountain is south of Tabor.

4. It is the northeastern spur of Mt. Ephraim.

5. North of this mountain Gideon defeated the Midianites.

No. 5.

1. This hill near Jerusalem is named from a common fruit tree.

2. Gethsemane is on its western slope.

3. Bethany and Bethphage are on its eastern side.

4. From its western side Christ viewed Jerusalem and wept over it.

5. Our Lord ascended from its summit.

No. 6.

1. A mountain east of Jericho, and east also of the Jordan.

2. From its peak, of another name, a great lawgiver viewed Canaan.

3. In the valley below this mountain Moses was buried.

4. North of it lay the territory of Sihon, king of the Amorites.

5. Balak and Balaam visited the top of this mountain.

No. 7.

1. A famous hill in Athens below the Acropolis.

2. The Greek name means the same as the English, being derived from Ares, god of war.

3. On this hill Paul delivered a notable address.

4. It was spoken before an informal gathering of philosophers.

5. Its text was an altar dedicated " to an unknown god."

No. 8.

1. The name of a mountain and also of an extensive mountainous district east of the Jordan.
2. The Jabbok cuts this district in two.
3. Elijah lived in this region.
4. The last interview between Jacob and Laban took place here.
5. The region was famous for its balm.

SERIES IX

Bible Trees

[Read each description a line at a time, and *Go Till You Guess.* Your score for each item is the number of the line at which you obtained the answer, and the lowest total wins.]

No. 1.

1. The leaves of this tree are of a dusty green, shaped like those of the privet.
2. Its leaves made the victor's crown in the Olympic games.
3. A branch of this tree is a symbol of peace.
4. A leaf from this tree brought cheer to Noah.
5. A valuable oil is obtained from its berries.
6. It gave its name to a famous hill near Jerusalem.

No. 2.

1. The prophet Amos worked on this kind of tree.
2. A certain tax-gatherer once utilized this tree.
3. The tree is sometimes 50 feet high and 60 feet broad.
4. It bears an edible fruit.
5. Its name signifies " the fig-mulberry."

No. 3.

1. Trees of this kind grew at Elim.

2. Branches (leaves) of this tree figured in a famous procession.
3. Under a tree of this kind dwelt a famous woman.
4. This tree was used in making booths for the feast of tabernacles.
5. Branches of this tree figure in heaven.
6. It is a beautiful and useful fruit tree.

No. 4.

1. Rebekah's nurse was buried under a tree of this kind.
2. Under this kind of tree Abraham first settled in Canaan.
3. Later, Abraham made a more permanent settlement under the same kind of tree.
4. At a tree of this kind Saul was saluted by three men.
5. This tree caused the death of Absalom.

No. 5.

1. A highly prized fruit tree, often mentioned with the grape-vine.
2. This tree was one of those invited to reign over the other trees.
3. Christ saw Nathanael under this tree.
4. Christ once caused this tree to wither away.
5. Christ drew from this tree a parable of the day of judgment.
6. James asks whether this tree can yield olives.

No. 6.

1. This tree grew with the cedar in Lebanon.
2. It was used, with cedar, for the woodwork of Solomon's temple.
3. It was used, according to Ezekiel, to make planks for ships.
4. Some of David's musical instruments were made from this tree.
5. The stork nested in its branches.
7. The tree is a conifer.

No. 7.

1. This is the most stately tree of the Bible.
2. Isaiah speaks of idols made from this tree.

3. Ezekiel mentions its use for masts.
4. It was much used in palaces and temples.
5. Its wood is very fragrant.
6. It was found in Lebanon.

SERIES X

Bible Daughters

[Read each description a line at a time, and *Go Till You Guess.* Your score for each item is the number of the line at which you obtained the answer, and the lowest total wins.]

No. 1.

1. This daughter was set to watch her baby brother on an important occasion.
2. She made a bright suggestion which affected his whole career.
3. She became a prophetess.
4. She grew jealous of her brother.
5. She was temporarily a leper.

No. 2.

1. She was the daughter of an adulterous queen.
2. Her mother was rebuked by a great prophet.
3. She used her daughter to contrive the prophet's death.
4. The daughter accomplished this by a dance.
5. The prophet was beheaded.

No. 3.

1. The Israelite women lamented this daughter's death four days every year.
2. She caused great sorrow to her father by going to meet him when he returned from war.
3. Her father was a mighty warrior.

4. He conquered the Ammonites.
5. He made a rash vow, which he kept.

No. 4.

1. This daughter comes upon the scene with a water pitcher on her shoulder.
2. She won a husband by being kind to a servant.
3. The servant took her a long journey to his master.
4. She had two sons, twins.
5. Her plotting brought her much sorrow.

No. 5.

1. This was one of seven daughters.
2. She lived in the Arabian desert east of the Red Sea.
3. Her father was a priest.
4. She married a brave stranger who watered her sheep for her.
5. She had two sons, Gershom and Eliezer.

No. 6.

1. Four unmarried daughters, in whose home Paul stayed for a time.
2. They were all prophetesses.
3. They lived in Cæsarea.
4. Their father was one of the seven deacons.
5. He is to be distinguished from an apostle of the same name.

No. 7.

1. She was the younger daughter of Laban.
2. She lived at Haran.
3. Her elder sister was substituted for her in marriage.
4. Jeremiah pictures her as weeping for her children.
5. She had two children, dying when the second was born.
6. She was buried near Bethlehem.

No. 8.

1. Her father gave her two springs for a marriage portion.
2. She married her uncle.
3. Her father was a heroic old man.
4. Her husband won her by taking a city.
5. Her father was one of the twelve spies.

No. 9.

1. She was the daughter of the greatest ruler of the times.
2. She found a baby as she went to bathe.
3. She named him from this circumstance.
4. She gave him the best education the world could afford.
5. He became the emancipator of his people.

No. 10.

1. She was the younger daughter of the first Israelite king.
2. She married the second Israelite king.
3. He won her by killing two hundred warriors.
4. She helped him escape from her father.
5. She rebuked him for his religious zeal.

SERIES XI

Bible Cities

[Read each description a line at a time, and *Go Till You Guess*. Your score for each item is the number of the line at which you obtained the answer, and the lowest total wins.]

No. 1.

1. Zedekiah was captured near this city.
2. Its rose plants were famous.

3. It was also famous for its palms.
4. There was a school of the prophets here.
5. This was the city of Rahab.
6. Its wall fell after thirteen encircling marches.

No. 2.

1. The name of this city means " a rolling," *i.e.*, the rolling away of reproach.

2. It was the first encampment of the Israelites after they crossed the Jordan.

3. At this city Saul transgressed by offering burnt offerings.

4. Here Saul was condemned for sparing Agag.

5. Here David was welcomed after the death of Absalom.

No. 3.

1. The original name of this city was Kirjath-arba.
2. Sarah died here.
3. At this place is the cave of Machpelah.
4. Caleb took possession of the city.
5. It was one of the cities of refuge.

No. 4.

1. This city was originally occupied by the Jebusites.
2. It was captured by David.
3. It was captured and laid waste by Nebuchadnezzar.
4. After fifty years the rebuilding was begun by Zerubbabel.
5. In A. D. 70 the city was captured and laid waste by the Romans under Titus.
6. Christ wept over this city.

No. 5.

1. The name means " the village of Nahum."

2. The city was Christ's headquarters.
3. The synagogue here was built by a Roman centurion.
4. Peter lived in this city.
5. Matthew was tax-collector here.
6. Here a palsied man was let down to Jesus through a roof.

No. 6.

1. This city is the most famous in the world for literature, art, and philosophy.
2. It is also famous for a visit made to it by the greatest Christian philosopher.
3. In the course of this visit he made a very notable address.
4. The address was based on an altar to " an unknown god."
5. The address emphasized Christ's resurrection.

No. 7.

1. Jonah's city of embarkation.
2. Place of entry of timber for Solomon's temple.
3. Home of Dorcas.
4. In this city Peter saw his vision of the descending sheet.
5. It is the seaport of Jerusalem.

No. 8.

1. A city of Africa founded by and named after a great conqueror.
2. Jews from this city had a synagogue in Jerusalem and joined in the persecution of Stephen.
3. Apollos came from this city.
4. Paul was shipwrecked in a vessel from this city.
5. Another ship from this city took Paul from Malta.
6. It was the second city of the Roman Empire.

No. 9.

1. This city was called Luz at first.

2. Its later name means " the house of God."
3. This was one of the cities where Samuel judged Israel.
4. Here was one of Jeroboam's centers of calf-worship.
5. Here Amos prophesied and was in danger of his life.

No. 10.

1. The king of this city was condemned by God to eat grass.
2. Jeremiah's prophecy that the city should " become heaps " was fulfilled.
3. Here a famous tower was built unto heaven.
4. Here a golden image was set up to be worshipped.
5. The city was famous for its hanging gardens.

No. 11.

1. The name means " the house of bread."
2. Near it Rachel died and was buried.
3. Boaz lived in this city.
4. Jesse also lived here.
5. David longed for the water of a well there.
6. It was the scene of a terrible massacre.

No. 12.

1. Joseph was cast into a pit near this town.
2. The town was near Shechem and Samaria.
3. Elisha was once besieged in this town.
4. Here was seen an encouraging vision of horses and fiery chariots.
5. Here the soldiers of a Syrian army were struck blind.

SERIES XII

Bible Objects

[Read each description a line at a time, and *Go Till You Guess*. Your score for each item is the number of the line at which you obtained the answer, and the lowest total wins.]

No. 1.

1. Part of this tool, falling into the water, was miraculously recovered by a prophet.

2. Abimelech used this tool when he set fire to the tower of Shechem.

3. The sound of this tool was not heard in Solomon's temple while it was building.

4. Isaiah asks whether this tool shall boast against him that uses it.

5. John the Baptist used this tool in his picture of coming judgment.

No. 2.

1. These receptacles were used for the heads of the seventy sons of Ahab whom Jehu had slain.

2. In one of his visions Amos saw summer fruit in this receptacle.

3. The chief baker told Joseph of a dream in which he had three of these receptacles on his head.

4. Paul was once put into this receptacle.

5. After one of Christ's miracles twelve of these receptacles were used.

No. 3.

1. This utensil was used by Gideon in his test of the meat and cakes.

2. It was promised in the Israelites' longing for Egypt.

3. One of them was kept in the ark.

4. The utensil figures in two of Elisha's helpful miracles.

5. Ecclesiastes uses it in a famous description of the laughter of fools.

No. 4.

1. Nehemiah's business had to do with this vessel.

2. This vessel was almost the undoing of Benjamin.

3. Christ condemned the hypocrites because they cleaned only the outside of this vessel.

4. Christ prayed that this vessel might pass from him.

5. David said that this vessel was running over.

No. 5.

1. Abraham carried this object in his hand on the way to Mount Moriah.

2. The Baal priests used it upon themselves in their wild worship on Mount Carmel.

3. A proverb of Agur speaks of a generation whose teeth are like this object " to devour the poor from off the earth."

4. Another proverb advises a man given to appetite to put this object to his throat.

No. 6.

1. One of these things was placed on the north side of the Holy Place.

2. One was placed in the prophet's chamber at Shunem.

3. A proverb speaks of one of these, owned by Wisdom, as being well furnished.

4. One of these, in the house of a rich man, is mentioned in the parable of Lazarus.

5. Some of these were once overturned by Christ.

No. 7.

1. Jael did her deadly deed with one of these objects (King James version).

2. Isaiah prophesies of Eliakim that he shall be like one of these objects fastened " in a sure place."

3. Isaiah speaks of these objects as used when " the carpenter encouraged the goldsmith."

4. The words of masters of assemblies are compared by Ecclesiastes to these objects.

5. The worst use of these objects was on Calvary.

No. 8.

1. Amos speaks of these things made of ivory.

2. Michal, to save David, took an image and laid it in this thing.

3. Christ asked whether a lamp should be put under one of these things.

4. One of these things was let down through the roof before Christ.

No. 9.

1. Manna is compared to this object.

2. It is so precious that the owner weeps when he parts with it.

3. The morning is the time to dispose of it.

4. Paul makes this object an emblem of the resurrection.

5. What was probably Christ's first parable is based on this object.

No. 10.

1. The passover was to be eaten with this object in hand.

2. This is all that Jacob had when he crossed the Jordan to go to Haran.

3. Zechariah had one of these that he named Beauty.

4. David had one of these in his hand as he advanced to meet Goliath.

5. Gehazi took this object from Elisha and ran with it to the Shunammite's dead son.

No. 11.

1. The transfer of this article was equivalent to the transfer of a right.

2. Removing these was a token of reverence.

3. Amos said that the rich men of Israel would sell the poor for two of these.

4. The Gibeonites used old articles of this sort to give the impression of long travel.

5. These were part of the father's gift to the prodigal on his return.

No. 12.

1. Rhoda is associated in memory with this object.

2. The Lord warned Cain that if he did not do well, sin would lie in wait here.

3. This object is connected with the ceremony of making a man a slave.

4. It is also prominent in the passover rites.

5. Christ called himself by the name of this object.

SERIES XIII

Bible Songs

[Read each description a line at a time, and *Go Till You Guess.* Your score for each item is the number of the line at which you obtained the answer, and the lowest total wins.]

No. 1.

1. This is the most famous song ever sung.
2. It was sung on the greatest of all occasions.
3. It was a birthday song.
4. It was two lines long.
5. The listeners were working men.
6. The singers were angels.

No. 2.

1. This song, by Moses, is in two parts.

2. It is a song of departure and return.

3. It is addressed to Jehovah as connected with a very sacred receptacle.

4. It was sung during the wilderness wanderings.

5. It was an appeal for guidance and protection.

No. 3.

1. A mother's song of the Old Testament.

2. This song declares: "Jehovah maketh poor, and maketh rich: He bringeth low, he also lifteth up."

3. It was sung by a woman who had been despised and scorned.

4. It was a song of triumph over the scorner.

5. It was a hymn of gratitude for prayer wonderfully answered.

No. 4.

1. This is the most beautiful song ever sung by a woman.

2. It celebrates the most wonderful event that ever happened to a woman.

3. The thought of the song is, "He hath exalted them of low degree."

4. The song was sung in the hill country of Judæa.

5. The song was sung in B. C. 5.

No. 5.

1. This song celebrates the bow of a noble warrior.

2. It is one of the most beautiful of all elegies.

3. It was sung by one of the world's greatest poets.

4. It lamented the death in battle of his dearest friend.

5. It contains the lines, "Thy love to me was wonderful, Passing the love of women."

No. 6.

1. This song celebrates the event which the Jews regarded as the most important in their history.

2. It was sung by the leader in that event.

3. The theme of the hymn is: "Jehovah is my strength and song, And he is become my salvation."

4. The song celebrates the most famous of all escapes.

5. The song was sung in the Sinai peninsula.

No. 7.

1. This song begins in the same way as the Beatitudes.

2. It was uttered by a priest who had been dumb.

3. It was sung in the hill country of Judæa.

4. It contained the prophecy, "The dayspring from on high shall visit us."

5. It concerned the priest's son who was to be a great prophet.

No. 8.

1. The song of a prophetess and a warrior.

2. It was sung to celebrate a victory.

3. It also celebrates the killing of a great warrior by a woman.

4. The warrior was slain with a tent-pin.

5   One line of the song is, "O my soul, march on with strength."

No. 9.

1. The song of the lawgiver of Israel.

2. It was sung just before his death.

3. It is recorded that his successor joined him in the song.

4. Many phrases of this song are in common use, such as "the finest of the wheat," "honey out of the rock," "waxed fat, and kicked."

5. The song is found in the fifth Book of the Pentateuch.

No. 10.

1. The song of a man who was "looking for the consolation of Israel."

2. The Holy Spirit had revealed to him that he should see the Messiah.

3. The song was sung in the temple.

4. It contained the phrase, "A light for revelation to the Gentiles."

5. It was sung before the sacrifice of " a pair of turtledoves or two young pigeons."

No. 11.

1. The song of a prophetess after Israel's greatest deliverance.

2. The song consisted of two lines.

3. The singer used a timbrel for her accompaniment.

4. She was followed as she marched by a crowd of women dancing with timbrels.

5. The first line of the song is, " Sing ye to Jehovah, for he hath triumphed gloriously."

No. 12.

1. The song of the greatest Hebrew singer on perhaps the happiest occasion of his life.

2. The song has to do with the establishment of worship in Jerusalem.

3. It has to do with a long-lost chest.

4. In it are the words, " Let the heavens be glad, and let the earth rejoice."

5. On the conclusion of the song, " all the people said, Amen, and praised Jehovah."

SERIES XIV

Bible Buildings

[Read each description a line at a time, and *Go Till You Guess*. Your score for each item is the number of the line at which you obtained the answer, and the lowest total wins.]

No. 1.

1. This building was erected by one of the greatest Jewish kings for his own use.

2. It required thirteen years to build.

3. It contained "the house of the forest of Lebanon," with many cedar pillars,—a room 150 feet long.

4. It contained a great ivory throne overlaid with gold.

5. It contained gorgeous apartments for an Egyptian princess.

6. It was in Jerusalem.

No. 2.

1. A movable place of worship in the shape of a great tent.

2. It contained two rooms, one square, the other oblong.

3. The square room was entirely closed by a heavy curtain, and contained one most sacred object.

4. The oblong room was entered daily by the priests and contained three objects.

5. The court surrounding the tent contained two objects.

No. 3.

1. This temple in Ephesus was one of the seven wonders of the world.

2. It served as a vast treasury and place of deposit for wealth.

3. It was four times as large as the Parthenon at Athens.

4. It was 342½ feet long and 164 feet wide.

5. It had a hundred columns 55 feet high, each made from one block of marble.

6. It was splendidly adorned by the greatest Grecian sculptors.

No. 4.

1. This was a castle in Jerusalem.

2. It adjoined the temple on the northwest.

3. It was named in honor of Marc Antony.

4. A Roman legion was stationed here to keep order in Jerusalem, especially during festivals.

5. Paul once addressed a mob from the stairs of this building.

No. 5.

1. This building in Jerusalem was one of the seven wonders of the world.

2. It cost nearly two and one-half billion dollars.

3. It was planned by one king and built by another with the aid of a third.

4. The entire interior was overlaid with gold.

5. It lasted four centuries and was destroyed by Nebuchadnezzar.

No. 6.

1. This was a lofty structure begun soon after the flood.

2. It was built of bricks cemented with bitumen.

3. The purpose of the structure was to establish a center for a centralized world power.

4. This ambitious purpose was frustrated by the rise of language difficulties.

5. A great city long afterwards rose at this place and took the name of this building.

No. 7.

1. This was a great building which Samson destroyed.
2. It was erected in honor of the national god of the Philistines.
3. Samson, blinded, pulled it down during a religious festival when it was crowded.
4. Some three thousand persons were on the roof.
5. Samson perished with the multitude.

No. 8.

1. This was a great edifice begun by Zerubbabel.
2. The building was authorized by Cyrus.
3. It was greatly hindered by the Samaritans.
4. Finally it was completed because of the urging of two prophets.
5. It was larger than its predecessor on the same site, but far less magnificent.
6. It lasted for five centuries.

No. 9.

1. Two cities built by a nation of slaves for their oppressors.
2. They were built of brick, which the slaves had to manufacture.
3. They were compelled to go out and gather straw to bind the brick.
4. Cruel taskmasters whipped them on in their work.
5. They were cities of granaries.

No. 10.

1. This was the third great building on the same site.
2. It was built by the king of Judæa just before the birth of Christ.
3. At the time of Christ's death a great earthquake worked destruction in this building.
4. It was not completely finished until eighty-two years.
5. It lasted only eighty-nine years.

SERIES XV

Bible Widows

[Read each description a line at a time, and *Go Till You Guess*. Your score for each item is the number of the line at which you obtained the answer, and the lowest total wins.]

No. 1.

1. This widow lived in a terrible famine.
2. She had only a little meal and oil left for herself and her son
3. She lived in Zarephath.
4. She responded to the appeal of a prophet.
5. As a result her food supply was miraculously continued.

No. 2.

1. A very old woman who had been a widow for eighty-four years
2. She was a prophetess.
3. She spent her time in the temple.
4. She recognized the infant Jesus as the Messiah.
5. She announced her discovery to many others.

No. 3.

1. She was the mother of a famed artificer.
2. She was born in Dan but lived in Naphtali.
3. Her dead husband was a Tyrian.
4. Her son may have been named after the king of Tyre.
5. He made the bronze work for Solomon's temple.

No. 4.

1. This widow was once watched by Jesus.

2. She was putting her gift into the temple receptacle for the purpose.

3. It was all she had, two little coins worth an eighth of a cent each.

4. Many rich people were making very large gifts.

5. Jesus said that the poor widow had given more than all the others.

No. 5.

1. This widow lost an only son.

2. Jesus saw the funeral procession.

3. He said to her, " Weep not."

4. He bade the corpse arise, and the young man sat up and began to speak.

5. Great fame came to Jesus because of this miracle.

No. 6.

1. The widow of one of Christ's parables.

2. The parable teaches earnestness in prayer.

3. The widow had been wronged and sought for justice.

4. The judge refused her at first, but was worn out by her persistent pleas.

5. " God," said Jesus, " is better than that judge."

No. 7.

1. This widow had lost her husband in a strange land.

2. She also lost her two sons.

3. She was cherished by one of her daughters-in-law.

4. With her she returned to her native land.

5. " Call me not ' Pleasant,' call me ' Bitter,' " she said.

No. 8.

1. This widow was threatened by her creditors, who were going to make slaves of her two children for debt.

2.   She had no possession but a pot of oil.

3.   She went to a great prophet who told her to borrow many empty vessels from her neighbors.

4.   These vessels were miraculously filled from her one pot of oil.

5.   She paid her debt and lived on what was left.

SERIES XVI

Bible Animals

[Read each description a line at a time, and *Go Till You Guess*. Your score for each item is the number of the line at which you obtained the answer, and the lowest total wins.]

No. 1.

1.   The family of Abdon the judge, seventy in number, all rode on these animals.

2.   Abigail rode on this animal to meet David.

3.   Balaam was rebuked by this animal.

4.   Zechariah prophesied of this animal in connection with the Messiah.

5.   Christ rode into Jerusalem on this animal.

No. 2.

1.   Herod Antipas was compared to this animal by Christ.

2.   This animal is said to spoil grapes.

3.   Nehemiah's enemies said that this animal could break down the wall he was building.

4.   Samson tied three hundred of them tail to tail.

5.   Christ referred to these animals in speaking of his own homelessness.

No. 3.

1. Isaiah compares the grief of his people over their disappointed hopes to the roar of this animal.

2. One of the proverbs says that meeting a fool in his folly is worse than meeting one of these animals robbed of her whelps.

3. Amos compares the day of God's condemnation to meeting one of these enraged beasts.

4. David told Saul that with his shepherd's club he had slain one of these beasts attacking his sheep.

5. When the lads of Bethel mocked Elisha, two of these animals tore to pieces forty-two of them.

No. 4.

1. The Hebrews were forbidden by law to muzzle this animal when engaged in threshing grain.

2. Isaiah foretold a time when the lion would eat straw like this animal.

3. Two of these animals of their own accord brought the ark back from the Philistines.

4. Elisha was using twenty-four of these animals when called to be a prophet.

5. One of the guests in Christ's parable excused himself by saying that he had to make a trial of ten of these animals.

No. 5.

1. This animal is connected with the death of Jezebel.

2. Hazael compared himself to this animal when told that he should reign over Israel.

3. Christ bids us not to give holy things to this animal.

4. A mother won a great boon from Christ by her shrewd mention of this animal.

5. In one of Christ's parables this animal is introduced as showing pity.

No. 6.

1.   The psalmist says that this animal is " a vain thing for safety."
2.   Job says of this animal, " He smelleth the battle afar off."
3.   Zechariah foretold the time when " Holiness unto Jehovah " should be engraved on the bells of this animal.
4.   This animal played a conspicuous part in the pursuit of the Israelites in the Exodus.
5.   This animal is connected with Jehu.

No. 7.

1.   The sluggard says that this animal is in the street.
2.   Samson made a riddle out of a carcass of this animal.
3.   A great Hebrew prophet was miraculously delivered from these beasts.
4.   Ecclesiastes says that a living dog is better than this animal dead.
5.   In the Revelation Christ is compared to this animal.

No. 8.

1.   A beautiful woman without discretion is compared to a ring of gold in the snout of this animal.
2.   The flesh of this animal was forbidden to the Jews.
3.   Christ forbade us to cast our pearls before this animal.
4.   In one of Christ's miracles a herd of these animals was caused to rush into the sea.
5.   In one of Christ's parables a young man is reduced to tending these animals.

No. 9.

1.   Amos took care of these animals.
2.   The greatest of the Hebrew kings took charge of these animals.
3.   The greatest event in the world's history was announced to men who were watching over these animals.

4. Isaiah said that the Messiah should be like one who tends these animals.

5. Christ adopted the prophecy for himself.

No. 10.

1. The hair of this animal furnished the covering for the tabernacle.

2. The young of this animal aided Jacob in his deception of Isaac.

3. This animal entered into the complaint of the prodigal's elder brother.

4. Gideon prepared this animal as food for the angel.

5. Christ compared this animal to the ungodly.

No. 11.

1. The Ishmaelites, who carried Joseph to Egypt, were using this animal.

2. Rebekah rode this animal to meet Isaac.

3. The coat of John the Baptist was made of this animal's hair.

4. The Queen of Sheba brought her presents to Solomon on these animals.

5. Christ said it was easier for this animal to go through a needle's eye than for a rich man to enter the kingdom of God.

No. 12.

1. Zephaniah compares corrupt judges to these animals; " they leave nothing till the morrow."

2. Isaiah says that in the Messiah's kingdom this animal " shall dwell with the lamb."

3. Paul at Miletus said that he knew that after his departure these animals would prey on the Christians, " not sparing the flock."

4. Christ sent the apostles forth as sheep in the midst of these animals.

5. Christ bade his followers beware of false prophets wearing sheep's clothing while inwardly they would be these animals.

SERIES XVII

Bible "Almosts"

[Read each description a line at a time, and *Go Till You Guess*. Your score for each item is the number of the line at which you obtained the answer, and the lowest total wins.]

No. 1.

1. He was a secret disciple, for fear of the Jews.
2. He was a member of the Sanhedrin.
3. He was rich.
4. He did not vote for Christ's condemnation.
5. He buried Jesus in his own new tomb.

No. 2.

1. A prophet's servant who would have thrust away a sorrowing mother.
2. He made an unsuccessful attempt to revive a dead boy.
3. He practised graft when his master healed a rich man.
4. He lied to his master about it.
5. For punishment he became a leper.

No. 3.

1. Of him it was said that " Jesus looking upon him loved him."
2. He asked, " What shall I do that I may inherit eternal life? "
3. Jesus said to him, " One thing thou lackest."
4. Jesus offered him treasure in heaven.
5. He did not accept Christ's challenge.

No. 4.

1. The first governor of Judæa before whom Paul was brought.
2. He made an ungodly union with Drusilla.

3. Paul preached before him so powerfully that he trembled.

4. He kept Paul for two years in his prison at Cæsarea.

5. He was looking for a bribe from Paul.

No. 5.

1. He was a Pharisee who had an important conversation with Christ by night.

2. He was a member of the Sanhedrin.

3. He protested against judging Christ unheard.

4. He aided in the burial of Jesus.

5. His name means " victor over the people."

No. 6.

1. A soothsayer, who lived on the Euphrates.

2. He saw Jehovah in his way, with a sword in his hand.

3. He said, " There shall come forth a star out of Jacob, and a sceptre shall rise out of Israel."

4. He refused rich rewards to curse Israel.

5. His ass spoke to him.

6. His counsel led the Israelites into idolatry, and so he was slain.

No. 7.

1. He slew a thousand men with the jawbone of an ass.

2. He was a Nazirite, and was invincible while observing his vow, letting his hair remain long.

3. He picked up a city gate and carried it off.

4. He was the slave of passion, and betrayed his secret of strength to a bad woman.

5. Blinded, he pulled down a heathen temple.

No. 8.

1. His advice " was as if a man inquired at the oracle of God."

2. He was one of David's counsellors.
3. He was the father of one of David's mighty men.
4. He went over to Absalom in his rebellion against David.
5. When his wise advice was not followed, he committed suicide.

SERIES XVIII

Bible Insects
And Other Small Animals

[Read each description a line at a time, and *Go Till You Guess.* Your score for each item is the number of the line at which you obtained the answer, and the lowest total wins.]

No. 1.

1. These insects are said to be " a people not strong, yet they provide their food in the summer."
2. The sluggard is advised to go to this insect, " consider her ways and be wise."

No. 2.

1. The Lord promised to send this insect before the Israelites, to drive out the Hivite, the Canaanite, and the Hittite.
2. Moses declared that God would send this insect among all the peoples of whom the Israelites were afraid.
3. Joshua said that God had sent this insect before his soldiers, driving out the two kings of the Amorites, " not with sword, nor with bow."

No. 3.

1. Isaiah prophesied that the Lord would hiss for this insect " that is in the land of Assyria."
2. The psalmist says that the nations compassed him about like these insects.

3.   Jonathan almost lost his life by eating the product of this insect.

4.   Deborah was named after this insect.

5.   John the Baptist in the wilderness ate the product of this insect.

No. 4.

1.   Job says that the wicked man " buildeth his house as " this insect.

2.   Speaking of his adversaries, Isaiah said, " They all shall wax old as a garment," and this insect " shall eat them up."

3.   Christ bids us not to lay up treasures on the earth where they will be destroyed by this insect.

No. 5.

1.   Ecclesiastes says that these insects, when dead, " cause the oil of the perfumer to send forth an evil odor."

2.   Isaiah said that the Lord would " hiss for " this insect " that is in the uttermost part of the rivers of Egypt."

3.   One of the plagues of Egypt was of these insects.

4.   One of the names of Satan is based on this insect.

No. 6.

1.   Joel wrote a magnificent description of this insect.

2.   John the Baptist ate it.

3.   It constituted one of the plagues of Egypt.

No. 7.

1.   The report of the ten spies spoke of the giants in Canaan, " and we were in our own sight as " these insects.

2.   Isaiah pictures God as sitting " above the circle of the earth, and the inhabitants thereof are as " these insects.

3.   Ecclesiastes describes old age as the time when this insect " shall be a burden."

No. 8.

1.   In one of the proverbs (King James version) it is said that this creature " taketh hold with her hands, yet is she in king's palaces."

2.   We read in Job that the trust of the godless man is like the frail construction made by this creature.

3.   Isaiah says of evil men that they hatch adders' eggs and weave the web of this creature.

No. 9.

1.   In the Revelation John saw creatures like these coming up out of the pit, striking " such men as have not the seal of God on their fore-heads."

2.   This creature was in " the great and terrible wilderness " of the forty years' wandering.

3.   Rehoboam said to the people that his father had chastised them with whips, but he would chastise them with these creatures.

4.   Christ gave his apostles power to tread on these creatures with impunity.

5.   Christ asked whether a father, if his son asked for an egg, would give him this creature.

SERIES XIX

More Bible Mountains

[Read each description a line at a time, and *Go Till You Guess*. Your score for each item is the number of the line at which you obtained the answer, and the lowest total wins.]

No. 1.

1.   This is the highest mountain of Palestine.

2.   It is the source of the Jordan, in the extreme north of Palestine.

3.   On one of its slopes probably occurred the transfiguration.
4.   It is 9,166 feet above the sea.
5.   Its summit is covered with perpetual snow.

No. 2.

1.   On the top of this mountain Eleazar was made high priest.
2.   The mountain was situated on the border of the land of Edom.
3.   Soon after leaving this mountain came the episode of the brazen serpent.
4.   On the top of this mountain Aaron died.
5.   At this mountain the Israelites mourned for Aaron thirty days.

No. 3.

1.   The name of the most sacred of all mountains.
2.   This hill was the abiding place of the ark.
3.   It was the hill on which the temple stood.
4.   The name of the hill came to be applied to all Jerusalem.
5.   The exact site of the original hill is in dispute: probably southeastern Jerusalem, though some say southwestern, and some even northwestern.

No. 4.

1.   This mountain was the northwestern boundary of Canaan.
2.   It is a double range, separated by a valley, running north and south.
3.   Mt. Hermon is a southern summit of the eastern range.
4.   The range was chiefly famous for its forests of great cedar trees.
5.   Cedar from this region was used in Solomon's temple.

No. 5.

1.   On this mountain occurred the most important event of the Old Testament.

2. The mountain has two names, used interchangeably.
3. It is situated between the two northern arms of the Red Sea.
4. Moses led his flock to pastures near this mountain.
5. On this mountain Elijah received a revelation from Jehovah.

No. 6.

1. Two mountains to the north and south of Shechem.
2. On the southern mountain was the temple of the Samaritans.
3. This is the mountain referred to in Christ's conversation at Jacob's well.
4. On the southern mountain Jotham proclaimed his parable to the men of Shechem.
5. Representatives of six tribes stood on one mountain and representatives of the other six tribes stood on the other mountain, pronouncing the blessings and curses.

No. 7.

1. This mountain is the traditional scene of Christ's temptation.
2. Its name is Latin meaning " Forty Days."
3. The name refers to the length of Christ's fast, supposed to have been spent in one of its caves.
4. The mountain is near Jericho.
5. It is part of the wilderness of Judæa, where John the Baptist lived.

No. 8.

1. This may be called, in allusion to the words spoken on it, the most " blessed " mountain in the world.
2. It is the traditional hill where the Sermon on the Mount was delivered.
3. It is square-shaped, with two tops.
4. It is about sixty feet high.
5. It is two or three miles west of the Sea of Galilee and seven miles southwest of Capernaum.

SERIES XX

Bible Miracles

[Read each description a line at a time, and *Go Till You Guess*. Your score for each item is the number of the line at which you obtained the answer, and the lowest total wins.]

No. 1.

1.   This, one of the three greatest miracles worked by Christ, was worked probably at Capernaum.

2.   Besides Christ, three apostles were present, and also one other man and woman.

3.   The miracle was worked at the request of a ruler of a synagogue.

4.   Just before the miracle Christ spoke of death as a sleep.

5.   In working the miracle Christ spoke two Aramaic words.

No. 2.

1.   This miracle was worked in connection with the removal of a theological seminary.

2.   The miracle exerted a power contrary to that of gravity.

3.   It was worked for the recovery of a borrowed tool.

4.   It was worked by throwing a stick into the water.

5.   It was worked by Elijah's successor.

No. 3.

1.   This miracle was worked at a temple door.

2.   It was worked by a man who had no silver or gold.

3.   It was worked in the name of Christ.

4.   It was worked for a beggar.

5.   The beneficiary of the miracle immediately went leaping into the temple, praising God.

No. 4.

1. This miracle was worked by the greatest man of the Old Testament.
2. It made use of certain devouring insects.
3. It also used a wonderful rod.
4. Its purpose was to soften a hard heart.
5. It did not succeed in this purpose.

No. 5.

1. This miracle overcame one of the mightiest forces of nature.
2. The people for whom it was worked were in imminent peril of death.
3. The worker of the miracle had been sleeping through the danger.
4. After working the miracle he asked, " Where is your faith? "
5. The miracle was worked on the Sea of Galilee.

No. 6.

1. This was Christ's only miracle of destruction.
2. The miracle covered two days.
3. The miracle was worked on Olivet.
4. In connection with the miracle Christ declared the omnipotence of faith.
5. The miracle was worked on a fruit tree.

No. 7.

1. This miracle was worked in connection with a procession.
2. It was a procession repeated thirteen times.
3. It was also connected with shouting and trumpets.
4. The miracle was worked on a fortification.
5. It took place in the days of Moses' successor.

No. 8.

1. This is the last recorded miracle of Jesus.

2.   It was worked in order to correct an error.

3.   It was worked for the benefit of two men, one of them being Christ's chief apostle.

4.   The other was a priest's servant.

5.   The miracle was worked in Gethsemane.

No. 9.

1.   This miracle was worked during the first missionary journey.

2.   It was worked by the leader of the expedition.

3.   It took place at Paphos.

4.   It was worked in order to punish opposition.

5.   It was worked upon a sorcerer.

No. 10.

1.   This was "the beginning of his signs."

2.   It was worked to supply an embarrassing lack.

3.   It was a transformation miracle.

4.   The material of the miracle was water.

5.   The miracle was worked at a wedding.

No. 11.

1.   This was a miracle of increase worked for a poor widow.

2.   It was worked by "the prophet of fire."

3.   It was worked in a time of famine.

4.   It was worked upon common foods.

5.   It took place at Zarephath.

No. 12.

1.   This was Christ's greatest miracle.

2.   It was worked for three friends.

3.   Christ deliberately delayed two days in working the miracle.

4.   In working it Christ declared, "I am the resurrection, and the life."

5.   The miracle took place at Bethany.

SERIES XXI

Another Company of Kings

[Read each description a line at a time, and *Go Till You Guess*. Your score for each item is the number of the line at which you obtained the answer, and the lowest total wins.]

No. 1.

1. The shepherd who became a king.
2. He captured for the Jews what became their chief city.
3. His dearest ambition was forbidden him.
4. He won a great victory with a pebble.
5. He wrote the most beloved of all lyrics.

No. 2.

1. This king began his reign by repairing and cleansing the temple.
2. Isaiah was his trusted friend and adviser.
3. He recovered from a severe sickness in answer to prayer.
4. God gave him a wonderful deliverance from the Assyrians, who were smitten with a sudden plague.
5. Hosea and Micah as well as Isaiah were his contemporaries.

No. 3.

1. The king under whom Babylon was captured.
2. He used in an impious feast the sacred vessels from Solomon's temple.
3. He was told supernaturally that he had been "weighed and found wanting."
4. In his reign the waters of the Euphrates were impounded.
5. His city was captured by one of Cyrus's generals.

No. 4.

1. He was king of Judæa in B. C. 5.
2. His family ruled Palestine, in whole or part, for five generations.
3. He had ten wives.
4. He is called " the Great."
5. He ordered the massacre of the Bethlehem children.

No. 5.

1. Three Books of the Old Testament are popularly attributed to him, also two psalms.
2. He was very learned, sagacious, and rich.
3. He was a famous builder.
4. He had a thousand women in his harem.
5. He was also called Jedidiah.

No. 6.

1. This Persian king was called " the Great."
2. Isaiah prophesied of his power and of his favor to the Jews.
3. He issued a proclamation allowing the Jews to return from exile to Palestine.
4. This proclamation brought about the first return under Zerubbabel (Sheshbazzar).
5. It was his general who captured Babylon.

No. 7.

1. This king set up calf-worship in Bethel and Dan.
2. He was of the tribe of Ephraim.
3. He was an able overseer of building operations.
4. A prophet foretold that he would be king over ten tribes.
5. To escape the wrath of his sovereign he fled to Egypt.

No. 8.

1. This king, when diseased in the feet, sought help from physicians but not from the Lord.

2. He removed the queen mother from her position because of her idolatry.

3. He was saved by prayer in a great invasion of Egyptians.

4. To get help from Syria against the Northern Kingdom he took the temple treasures.

5. He opened his reign with a vigorous campaign against idolatry.

No. 9.

1. This king had a nickname derived from his hands.

2. When Zerubbabel was rebuilding Jerusalem, this king was led to forbid it.

3. Afterwards he permitted it.

4. He allowed Ezra to take a company of exiles back to Jerusalem.

5. Nehemiah was his cupbearer.

No. 10.

1. The last thing this king saw was the slaughter of his sons.

2. He sent secretly for a great prophet, to get his advice.

3. He had another secret interview with the same prophet in the temple.

4. He passed through probably the most terrible siege known up to that time.

5. He was carried in chains to Babylon.

No. 11.

1. This king treated savagely a nation of slaves.

2. He was a great warrior, carrying his campaigns into Asia Minor and nearly to the Tigris.

3. He established libraries and schools.

4.   He used his Jewish slaves in building Pa-ramses and Pithom.

5.   His mummy is now to be seen in Egypt.

No. 12.

1.   This king of Israel married a heathen princess whose wickedness has become proverbial.

2.   His powerful opponent was " the prophet of fire."

3.   His wife had a far stronger will than he had.

4.   She obtained for him, by a murder under the forms of law, a vineyard he greatly desired.

5.   He was killed in battle by a soldier who drew his bow at a venture.

SERIES XXII

Bible Sayings

[Read each description a line at a time, and *Go Till You Guess*. Your score for each item is the number of the line at which you obtained the answer, and the lowest total wins.]

No. 1.

1.   An often-quoted sentence by Nathan.

2.   It was spoken in rebuke of a king.

3.   The king had committed a double crime.

4.   The sentence was the " snapper " of a parable.

5.   It is often used to drive home a condemnation.

No. 2.

1.   This was spoken in connection with Christ's greatest miracle.

2.   It was spoken to a sorrowing woman.

3.   It was spoken in a little village which he loved to visit.

4.   It was spoken with reference to a friend's death.

5.   It is often quoted in funeral services.

No. 3.

1. The question asked by the "prophet of fire" at the most dramatic moment of his life.
2. The question was asked of the crowd of spectators.
3. The question was asked standing on a mountain.
4. Many of his hearers were idolaters.
5. He was about to demonstrate by a tremendous test the power of his God.

No. 4.

1. A question asked by a jailer.
2. The most important question any one can ask.
3. It was asked after a very thrilling event.
4. The place was a famous Greek city.
5. The question was asked of two missionaries.

No. 5.

1. The most beautiful one-sentence prayer ever uttered.
2. It was spoken under the most terrible circumstances.
3. It was spoken just outside of Jerusalem.
4. It was uttered by the person referred to in Isa. 53.
5. It was a petition on behalf of those whom one would least expect to be prayed for.

No. 6.

1. A heartless question asked at the beginning of history.
2. It was asked by the first farmer.
3. It was asked after he had committed a terrible sin.
4. It implied a negative answer.
5. It should always have an affirmative reply.

No. 7.

1. A sentence about fidelity and a crown.

2.   It was sent to the Christians of Smyrna.

3.   It was sent by the Son of Man.

4.   It is in one of seven little letters.

5.   It is in the last Book of the Bible.

No. 8.

1.   This sentence was spoken by a man on a wall.

2.   It was spoken by a very brave and determined man.

3.   He had come nine hundred miles to do a certain thing.

4.   The sentence was spoken to men who sought to prevent his doing that thing.

5.   He did it.

No. 9.

1.   Perhaps the most beautiful of all expressions of resignation.

2.   It was spoken by a man who had been rich but had lost all his wealth.

3.   He had also lost all his dear ones.

4.   He was in terrible bodily plight.

5.   And all this was brought upon him to test his faith in God.

SERIES XXIII

Bible Soldiers

[Read each description a line at a time, and *Go Till You Guess.* Your score for each item is the number of the line at which you obtained the answer, and the lowest total wins.]

No. 1.

1.   His father was Nun.

2.   He defeated the Amalekites in Rephidim.

3. He was the successor of the greatest man of the Old Testament.

4. The Lord said to him, " I will not fail thee, nor forsake thee. Be strong and of good courage."

5. He led the Israelites in the conquest of Canaan.

No. 2.

1. He was cupbearer to a king.

2. His brother was Hanani.

3. He said, " The God of heaven, he will prosper us; therefore we his servants will arise and build."

4. He said, " The people had a mind to work."

5. He said, " Should such a man as I flee? "

No. 3.

1. He was the commander of the army of the king of Damascus.

2. He was a leper.

3. He was helped by a little captive girl.

4. He was helped by a great Hebrew prophet.

5. At first he scorned the cure that was offered him.

No. 4.

1. He was the son of Jephunneh.

2. He took part in the exploration of Canaan.

3. He and one other made a famous minority report.

4. He captured Hebron when he was eighty-five years old.

5. He was the father of Achsah.

No. 5.

1. A very big man who lived in Gath.

2. His coat of mail weighed 157 pounds.

3. He was more than ten feet high.

4. He shouted, "Am I a dog, that thou comest to me with staves? "

5. He was slain with a pebble.

No. 6.

1. He said, " Only say the word, and my servant shall be healed."
2. He built a synagogue for the Jews.
3. He spoke to Christ of his authority.
4. He was a Roman.
5. Christ said he had more faith than any Jew.

No. 7.

1. With only his armor-bearer he climbed a cliff and attacked an army.
2. He came near losing his life on account of some honey.
3. At one time his father tried to kill him.
4. A great poet was his best friend.
5. When he died, the poet sang, " Thy love to me was wonderful, passing the love of women."

No. 8.

1. One of his names was Jerubbaal.
2. He received a confirmatory sign by means of a fleece of wool.
3. He cut his army down from thirty-two thousand men to three hundred.
4. He terrified the enemy with trumpets, torches, and pitchers.
5. He has been called the greatest of the Judges.

No. 9.

1. He was a Hittite, greatly wronged by a Jew.
2. Recalled from war, he refused to go to his home, but slept with the king's servants.
3. The king made him drunk, but still he would not go to his home.
4. The king had him exposed in the hottest part of the battle, so that he was slain.
5. His wife became the mother of Solomon.

No. 10.

1. The Gileadite who conquered the Ammonites.
2. He was driven from Gilead and became an outlaw.
3. The Gileadites were compelled to ask him to become their chief.
4. He made a rash vow, which involved his only child, a noble young woman.
5. He was for six years a judge of Israel.

SERIES XXIV

Bible Prophets

[Read each description a line at a time, and *Go Till You Guess*. Your score for each item is the number of the line at which you obtained the answer, and the lowest total wins.]

No. 1.

1. He was a farmer and a shepherd.
2. Part of his duty was to tend sycomore trees.
3. He lived in Tekoa.
4. His business carried him to Bethel.
5. His bold utterances there put him in peril.

No. 2.

1. He uttered the *Nunc dimittis.*
2. He was " looking for the consolation of Israel."
3. He foretold Mary's heart-piercing sorrows.
4. He foretold that Christ should be " a sign which is spoken against."
5. He prophesied that Christ should be " a light for revelation to the Gentiles."

No. 3.

1. He was once protected by a ring of horses and chariots of fire.
2. He was instrumental in the healing of a leprous general.
3. He sweetened the waters of a spring.
4. He purified some poisonous pottage.
5. He fed a hundred men with twenty barley loaves and a few ears of corn.

No. 4.

1. He is often called " the last of the prophets."
2. He was a Nazirite.
3. He called the people to repent, for the kingdom of heaven was near.
4. He was ascetic in his manner of living.
5. He became the first martyr of New Testament times.

No. 5.

1. His home town was Anathoth.
2. A writing of his was cut to pieces with a penknife.
3. His great helper was Baruch.
4. He was once imprisoned in a well.
5. He is called " the weeping prophet."

No. 6.

1. He was a Christian prophet of Jerusalem.
2. He made a prediction in Antioch.
3. He made another prediction in Cæsarea.
4. He foretold the great famine in the reign of the emperor Claudius.
5. He foretold Paul's arrest in Jerusalem.

No. 7.

1. This prophet made a striking use of locusts in his Book.
2. His writings are a call to repentance with an account of the bless-ings it brings.
3. He bade the people, " Rend your heart, and not your garments."
4. He said, " My people shall never be put to shame."
5. He is the second of the Minor Prophets.

No. 8.

1. He rose to great power in the land of the exile.
2. He was an interpreter of dreams.
3. He was also a profound seer of the future.
4. He once recited a dream which the dreamer himself had forgotten.
5. He was preserved when thrown to the lions.

No. 9.

1. He was the tenth of the Minor Prophets.
2. He urged the rebuilding of the temple, which had halted for fifteen years.
3. He prophesied in the time of Zerubbabel.
4. One of his striking sentences is, " He that earneth wages earneth wages to put it into a bag with holes."
5. Another is, " The silver is mine, and the gold is mine, saith the Lord of hosts."

No. 10.

1. This prophet, after a great victory, ran away from a woman.
2. He was a Tishbite.
3. Birds brought him food.
4. He brought down fire from heaven.
5. He went to heaven without dying.

No. 11.

1. This prophet ran away from God's summons to a difficult task.
2. A terrible storm made him see his duty.
3. He was the subject of the most discussed miracle of the Old Testament.
4. He prophesied in the greatest city of his time.
5. A plant became to him a sermon on the loving care of Jehovah.

No. 12.

1. A prophet who tore his robe into twelve pieces.
2. He lived in Shiloh.
3. He prophesied to Jeroboam.
4. His prophecy was instrumental in dividing a kingdom.
5. Though half-blind, he recognized a queen who came to him in disguise.

SERIES XXV

Bible Children

[Read each description a line at a time, and *Go Till You Guess*. Your score for each item is the number of the line at which you obtained the answer, and the lowest total wins.]

No. 1.

1. This was a little Jewish girl who was a captive.
2. She had been captured by Syrian soldiers.
3. She was slave to the wife of a great general.
4. He was suffering a terrible disease.
5. The little girl told about a great Jewish prophet who was able to heal, and thus the general was cured of his disease.

No. 2.

1. Paul called him " my child," " my true child in faith," " my beloved child."

2. Paul bade him, " Let no man despise thy youth."

3. Paul reminded him of the godly faith of his mother and grandmother.

4. Paul bade him be true to his childhood's Bible studies.

5. He was Paul's best-loved helper.

No. 3.

1. His mother obeyed the king's command to cast every man-child into the river—in the letter but not in the spirit.

2. The child was saved through the loving thought of his mother and sister.

3. He was adopted by a princess.

4. He received a splendid education.

5. He became the savior of his people.

No. 4.

1. A boy whose lunch was the basis of a great feast.

2. He had only two little fishes and five flat, thin barley cakes.

3. With them five thousand men were fed.

4. Twelve baskets of fragments were left over.

5. This happened northeast of the Sea of Galilee.

No. 5.

1. " I am but a little child," said this prince as he succeeded to a great kingdom.

2. He had a dream in which God offered him anything he might choose.

3. He chose wisdom, that he might know how to rule.

4. God gave it in abundance, and added riches and honor.

5. In addition God promised him a long life, if he would keep his commandments.

No. 6.

1. She was a young servant of Mary, the mother of John Mark.
2. They were holding a prayer meeting in Mary's house.
3. The girl answered a knock at the door.
4. She thought the person she found was a ghost.
5. Her name was "Rose."

No. 7.

1. A king who began to reign when he was only eight years old.
2. His mother was Jedidah.
3. He reigned in Jerusalem.
4. In his reign the Book of the Law was found in the temple.
5. He came to an untimely end in the battle of Megiddo.

No. 8.

1. This child spent his boyhood in the tabernacle.
2. He was dedicated to God because he came in answer to prayer.
3. He waited on a feeble old man.
4. God gave the boy a communication one night.
5. His mother brought him a special robe every year.

No. 9.

1. These were young lads who made fun of a great man.
2. The great man was a prophet.
3. The lads belonged to Bethel.
4. They shouted after the prophet, "Baldhead! Baldhead! Go up, you baldhead!"
5. Forty-two of the lads were punished by bears out of the wood.

No. 10.

1. This boy was called Belteshazzar in place of his Hebrew name.
2. He presented a petition to Ashpenaz.
3. He asked to be allowed to live on water and vegetables.
4. He objected to the wine and rich food which had been given him.
5. He became famous for his wisdom and rose to be next to the king himself.

No. 11.

1. This boy lived in Shunem.
2. His mother was a " great woman."
3. The son was given her as a reward for her kindness to a prophet.
4. One day in the harvest field the boy cried, " My head, my head! " and soon died.
5. The prophet brought him back to life.

No. 12.

1. This boy lived in Bethlehem.
2. He was the youngest of eight brothers.
3. His daily task was to tend sheep.
4. A great prophet solemnly poured oil on his head one day.
5. He became the greatest of Hebrew kings.

No. 13.

1. All the brothers and sisters of this boy were killed by his grandmother, who thereby became queen.
2. He was saved by his aunt.
3. For six years he was hidden in the temple.
4. Then his uncle plotted with the royal bodyguard, who slew the wicked queen.
5. So the boy became king, and did well while his uncle lived to advise him.

SERIES XXVI

Bible Queens

[Read each description a line at a time, and *Go Till You Guess*. Your score for each item is the number of the line at which you obtained the answer, and the lowest total wins.]

No. 1.

1. Of this queen it is recorded that she painted her eyes.
2. She slew many prophets.
3. She caused a great prophet to run away.
4. She caused the owner of a desired vineyard to be killed.
5. She was daughter of the king of the Sidonians and an idolater.
6. She was eaten by dogs.

No. 2.

1. Her Hebrew name means myrtle; her Persian name means a star.
2. Her deeds originated the feast of Purim (lots).
3. Her life was closely connected with her cousin's.
4. She was made queen in substitution for another queen.
5. The holding out of a sceptre saved her life.
6. She said, " If I perish, I perish."

No. 3.

1. This queen reigned in southwestern Arabia.
2. She is famous for a journey which she made.
3. Also for a great present which she gave.
4. Also for the questions which she asked.
5. Her story is told in connection with Solomon's.

No. 4.

1. She reigned six years in Israel.
2. She began her reign by killing all her grandsons but one.
3. One of her grandsons was saved by his aunt.
4. She was punished by a priest.
5. Her last recorded words were "Treason! Treason!"
6. She was slain at the carriage entrance of the palace.

No. 5.

1. She married the son of Mariamne.
2. She left him for his half-brother.
3. This half-brother divorced his lawful wife.
4. A great prophet reproved the guilty pair.
5. This queen procured the prophet's death.
6. She succeeded in this through her daughter's dancing.

No. 6.

1. Her husband was the most powerful monarch in the world.
2. He was drunk at a feast and ordered her to display her beauty before the company.
3. The queen indignantly refused.
4. For this refusal she was deposed.
5. Her husband was the Xerxes of secular history.

SERIES XXVII

Bible Men

[Read each description a line at a time, and *Go Till You Guess*. Your score for each item is the number of the line at which you obtained the answer, and the lowest total wins.]

No. 1.

1. A patriarch who lived in the land of Uz.

2.   The devil received permission to test his character.

3.   He met the many terrible calamities that Satan sent with the question: " What? shall we receive good at the hand of God, and shall we not receive evil? "

4.   His friends thought he must have been a great sinner and urged him to confess his sins.

5.   Finally Satan was defeated and the patriarch's fortunes were restored.

No. 2.

1.   The governor of the palace of a wicked king of Israel.

2.   He saved a hundred prophets by hiding them in a cave.

3.   He was sent to look for grass in the midst of a terrible drought.

4.   He met a great prophet who bade him arrange an interview with the king.

5.   This he undertook with extreme reluctance.

No. 3.

1.   A preacher of righteousness in a time of almost universal wickedness.

2.   The savior of a remnant in a time of almost universal destruction.

3.   The founder of a new world of men, animals, and plants.

4.   The builder of a great boat.

5.   And, alas! the first recorded drunkard.

No. 4.

1.   He took the ark into his house for three months.

2.   Others were afraid of it because a man had been struck dead for touching it irreverently.

3.   During the three months his house received many manifest blessings.

4. When this was known, the ark was taken the rest of its journey.
5. This was in the days of David.

No. 5.

1. He lied to the Holy Spirit.
2. He kept back part of the price.
3. He pretended that what he gave was the whole price.
4. Peter told him that Satan had filled his heart.
5. On hearing these words he fell down dead.

No. 6.

1. This man is connected with Rehoboth.
2. He was very fond of venison.
3. He was fooled by his son in his old age.
4. He was peaceable in regard to wells.
5. His wooing was done by proxy.

No. 7.

1. He is known to history because of his ear.
2. His right ear was cut off.
3. It was at once supernaturally healed.
4. This took place in a plot of ground known as the Oil Press.
5. The man who cut off the ear was Peter.

No. 8.

1. He walked with God.
2. He was the son of Jared.
3. He was the father of Methuselah.
4. He " was not, for God took him."
5. He had witness borne to him that he had been well-pleasing to God.

No. 9.

1. He was sent to the home of Judas.
2. He was sent to a man who was praying.
3. He was afraid to go, for the man was a persecutor.
4. The man who was praying had been blinded.
5. He was sent to restore his sight.

No. 10.

1. This man was famous for his long, fine hair.
2. He said, " Oh, that I were made judge in the land! "
3. He took the advice of Ahithophel.
4. His head was caught in the boughs of an oak.
5. His father lamented, " Would I had died for thee, my son, my son! "

No. 11.

1. He was the father of Alexander and Rufus.
2. He came from Cyrene.
3. He was going into Jerusalem from the country.
4. His name was the same as Peter's.
5. He was obliged to help Christ.

No. 12.

1. He was captured by Chedorlaomer.
2. He was the son of Haran.
3. He chose the Plain of the Jordan.
4. He was warned by two angels.
5. His wife became a pillar of salt.

SERIES XXVIII

Bible Women

[Read each description a line at a time, and *Go Till You Guess*. Your score for each item is the number of the line at which you obtained the answer, and the lowest total wins.]

No. 1.

1. She chose the one thing needful.
2. She broke an alabaster box for Jesus.
3. She sat at Christ's feet, listening.
4. Her brother died, and she was sure it would not have happened if Christ had been there.
5. She lived in a village on Olivet.

No. 2.

1. She was a prophetess in the time of the Judges.
2. Her name means a bee.
3. She lived under a palm-tree.
4. She allied herself with a general and won a great victory with him.
5. She celebrated it in a magnificent ode.

No. 3.

1. She was a dealer in purple cloth.
2. She came from Asia but lived in Europe.
3. She was won to Christ in an open-air meeting.
4. All her household were baptized with her.
5. One proof of her conversion was her hospitality.

No. 4.

1. She saved her nephew from his murderous grandmother.
2. She kept the young child hidden for six years in the temple.
3. She was the wife of a high priest.
4. Her husband plotted against the grandmother and had her executed.
5. Then the young child became king of the realm.

No. 5.

1. A deaconess specially commended by Paul.
2. She lived at Cenchreæ, the eastern port of Corinth.
3. Paul said that she had helped himself, and many others.
4. She is mentioned in the letter to the Romans.
5. It is probable that she carried that letter to Rome.

No. 6.

1. She was a disreputable woman of Jericho.
2. She is probably named among the ancestors of our Lord.
3. She became famous in Hebrew history by an act of kindness to two spies.
4. She acknowledged Jehovah to be the true God.
5. For these reasons the Hebrew conquerors saved and protected her.

No. 7.

1. She gave her name to women's charitable societies.
2. Her name means "gazelle."
3. Her Aramaic name was Tabitha.
4. She lived in Joppa.
5. When she died, they sent for Peter, who brought her back to life.

No. 8.

1. She came from a town on the western shore of the Sea of Galilee, about three miles north of Tiberias.

2. She was one of the women who followed Jesus, ministering to him of their substance.

3. Jesus drove seven demons out of her.

4. She was one of the women at the cross.

5. She was the first person to whom Christ appeared after his resurrection.

No. 9.

1. She was evidently a busy housekeeper.

2. She may have been the wife or widow of " Simon the leper."

3. Jesus was received at her house.

4. She believed in Christ's power to heal the sick.

5. Christ told her that she was over-anxious about many things.

No. 10.

1. She was the cause of one of Paul's imprisonments.

2. She had " a spirit of divination."

3. She was so profitable for fortune-telling that a company was formed to exploit her alleged powers.

4. She followed Paul so persistently with insane cries that he drove the demon out of her.

5. Thereupon her masters had Paul imprisoned.

SERIES XXIX

Bible Food and Drink

[Read each description a line at a time, and *Go Till You Guess*. Your score for each item is the number of the line at which you obtained the answer, and the lowest total wins.]

No. 1.

1. The prophetic roll which Ezekiel ate tasted like this food.

2. A proverb says that it is not good to eat much of it.
3. The manna tasted like it.
4. Jonathan came into grave danger because of it.
5. Samson made a riddle out of it.

No. 2.

1. The psalmist says that a wicked man's mouth is as smooth as this food.
2. This was one of the articles of food which Abraham set before the three angels.
3. Jael brought this food to Sisera " in a lordly dish."
4. When David fled before Absalom, this was one of the articles of food brought him by three loyal subjects.
5. In Job we read of " flowing streams of honey " and this food.

No. 3.

1. Abigail's present to David included two hundred cakes made of this fruit.
2. With a cake made of this fruit they fed the Egyptian found in a field who led David to the Amalekites.
3. Isaiah laid a cake of this fruit on Hezekiah's boil, and he recovered.
4. Nehemiah stopped the selling of this fruit in Jerusalem on the Sabbath.
5. Jeremiah had a vision of two baskets of this fruit, one good, the other bad.

No. 4.

1. Cakes mixed with this substance were required for the peace-offerings.
2. When the Almighty married Jerusalem, as Ezekiel said, he fed her with fine flour and honey and this substance.

3. Unleavened cakes mixed with this substance were used in the consecration of priests.

4. The manna tasted like this substance when it is fresh.

5. The prophet's widow whom Elisha helped had nothing in the house except a pot of this substance.

No. 5.

1. A proverb compares one who sings songs with a heavy heart to this liquid upon soda.

2. This liquid was forbidden to the Nazirite.

3. Boaz bade Ruth dip her bread in this liquid.

4. The sluggard on an errand is compared by a proverb to this liquid to the teeth.

5. This liquid was given to Christ on the cross.

No. 6.

1. Shammah defended from the Philistines a plot full of this vegetable.

2. Ezekiel was to make bread of this vegetable, with others, and eat it for three hundred and ninety days.

3. Barzillai brought this vegetable to David during Absalom's rebellion.

4. Esau sold his birthright for soup made of this vegetable.

No. 7.

1. David was sent with ten of this kind of food to his brothers' captain.

2. Barzillai brought this food to David in his flight from Absalom.

3. Job asked, " Hast thou not curdled me like " this food?

No. 8.

1. Christ asked whether a father, if his son asked for this food, would offer a scorpion.

2. Isaiah says that this food, derived from an adder, is poisonous.

3. Job asks whether there is any taste in the white portion of this food.

No. 9.

1. This food was set out before God in the tabernacle.

2. In the dream which Gideon overheard this food tumbled into the camp of the Midianites.

3. At Emmaus Christ was disclosed as he blessed this food.

4. Christ compared himself to this food.

5. One of Christ's miracles was the multiplication of this food.

No. 10.

1. Paul told the Corinthians that he had fed them with this.

2. Peter urged his readers to desire it, that they might " grow thereby unto salvation."

3. Jacob prophesied that Judah's teeth should be white with this.

4. Sisera asked for water, but Jael gave him this.

5. Isaiah called on every one to buy this " without money and without price."

No. 11.

1. Paul urged that speech should be mixed with this food.

2. Elisha healed the bad spring with this substance.

3. Artaxerxes gave Ezra this substance " without prescribing how much."

4. Christ compared Christians to this food.

5. Christ bade his followers to have this substance in themselves, " and be at peace one with another."

No. 12.

1. Because of the way in which Moses and Aaron obtained this at Meribah, they were shut out of the promised land.

2.   Elijah begged this from the widow of Zarephath.

3.   Jesus besought it from the woman of Samaria.

4.   David longed for some of it from Bethlehem.

5.   Christ promised a reward to one who would give only a little of it to one of his little ones.

SERIES XXX

Morĕ Bible Prophets

[Read each description a line at a time, and *Go Till You Guess.* Your score for each item is the number of the line at which you obtained the answer, and the lowest total wins.]

No. 1.

1.   This prophet set forth God's persistent love for his disobedient people by the analogy of a patient husband and an adulterous wife.

2.   He was probably the earliest of the Minor Prophets.

3.   One of his striking sentences: " My people are destroyed for lack of knowledge."

4.   Another sentence often quoted: " Ephraim is joined to idols; let him alone."

5.   Another: " They sow the wind, and they shall reap the whirlwind."

No. 2.

1.   This prophet's mouth was touched by a live coal from the altar.

2.   In answer to God's call for a messenger to the people, he said, " Here am I; send me."

3.   His father's name was Amoz.

4.   He was the mainstay of King Hezekiah.

5.   One of his sentences: " Seek ye the Lord while he may be found; call ye upon him while he is near."

No. 3.

1. He was a native of Moresheth-gath.

2. His writings are much like those of Isaiah.

3. He prophesied: "They shall beat their swords into plowshares, and their spears into pruning-hooks."

4. One of his questions: "What doth Jehovah require of thee, but to do justly, and to love kindness, and to walk humbly with thy God?"

5. Another sentence from this prophet: "They shall sit every man under his vine and under his fig-tree."

No. 4.

1. In order to have a parable for one of his sermons, this prophet cut off his hair and beard with a sharp sword.

2. One of his visions was of the valley of dry bones.

3. Another vision was of the chamber of imagery.

4. The expression, "Wheels within wheels," comes from this prophet.

5. He prophesied "among the captives by the river Chebar."

No. 5.

1. His name means "my messenger."

2. His prophecy includes a strong plea for tithing.

3. It closes with a prophecy of John the Baptist.

4. It speaks of God's "book of remembrance."

5. It includes God's promise, under certain conditions, to open the windows of heaven, and pour out such a blessing that there shall not be room to receive it.

No. 6.

1. He prophesied before two kings, greatly displeasing one of them.

2. His first prophecy was ironical, and he was asked to speak sincerely.

3. His second prophecy was unfavorable to the project under consideration, and he was thrown into prison.

4. About four hundred heathen prophets were present, prophesying favorably.

5. The event proved the one prophet of Jehovah to be right.

No. 7.

1. A prophet descended from King Hezekiah.

2. He prophesied in the reign of King Josiah.

3. He declared that " the great day of Jehovah" was near at hand.

4. He said, " Jehovah thy God is in the midst of thee, a mighty one who will save."

5. He said of God: " Every morning doth he bring his justice to light, he faileth not."

No. 8.

1. He is called the second founder of the Hebrew nation.

2. After Moses, he was the earliest of the great Hebrew prophets.

3. His father was Elkanah.

4. His stone of Ebenezer marked a great victory over the Philistines.

5. In his old age, he was forced by the people to appoint a king.

No. 9.

1. He was the son of Berechiah and grandson of Iddo.

2. He prophesied in the days of Zerubbabel.

3. He joined another prophet and stimulated the people to build the second temple.

4. His Book contains a series of eight wonderful visions.

5. It contains the prophecy of Christ: " In that day there shall be a fountain opened to the house of David and to the inhabitants of Jerusalem, for sin and for uncleanness."

No. 10.

1. He wrote the powerful temperance passage, beginning, "Woe unto him that giveth his neighbor drink."

2. He wrote the often-quoted words: "The Lord is in his holy temple: let all the earth keep silence before him."

3. His phrase, "that he may run that readeth it," is often misquoted.

4. His words are weighty: "The righteous shall live by his faith."

5. He wrote a beautiful psalm, and may have belonged to a guild of temple singers.

SERIES XXXI

Bible Prayers

[Read each description a line at a time, and *Go Till You Guess.* Your score for each item is the number of the line at which you obtained the answer, and the lowest total wins.]

No. 1.

1. Prayers made by a man with his windows open toward Jerusalem.

2. They were made three times a day.

3. They were made in disobedience to a king's command.

4. The man who offered the prayers came thereby into terrible danger.

5. The result was his safety and high honor to God.

No. 2.

1. This prayer, closing a heroic life, was like one of Christ's prayers on the cross.

2. It was prayed in a loud voice.

3. It was only a sentence long.

4. It showed a beautiful, forgiving spirit.

5. It was offered by one of the first deacons.

No. 3.

1. Announcement of this prayer was made to Ananias.

2. The prayer was made by a man who had been a great wrongdoer.

3. He had recently been converted.

4. In the event he had become blind.

5. Ananias was sent to restore his sight.

No. 4.

1. This prayer was prompted by a terrible threat from the king of Assyria.

2. The king of Judah " spread it before Jehovah."

3. He said, " Thou art the God, even thou alone, of all the kingdoms of the earth."

4. Isaiah assured him that God would defend Jerusalem.

5. In the morning the Assyrians " were all dead bodies."

No. 5.

1. This prayer occupies an entire chapter of one of the Gospels.

2. It contains the petition " that they may all be one."

3. It contains the sentence: " This is life eternal, that they should know thee the only true God, and him whom thou didst send, even Jesus Christ."

4. Also the sentence: " I pray not that thou shouldest take them from the world, but that thou shouldest keep them from the evil one."

5. The prayer was made in an upper room in Jerusalem.

No. 6.

1. This prayer was made in dedicating a building.

2. The one who offered it stood before an altar and spread forth his hands toward heaven.

3. The prayer begins: " O Jehovah, the God of Israel, there is no God like thee."

4. A refrain of the prayer is: " Hear thou in heaven thy dwelling-place; and when thou hearest, forgive."

5. The prayer was uttered by a great king.

No. 7.

1. This prayer was uttered by a man who had done great wrong and feared the coming of the man he had wronged.

2. The prayer said to God: " I am not worthy of the least of all the lovingkindnesses, and of all the truth, which thou hast showed unto thy servant."

3. It prayed for deliverance from the wronged man who was approaching, " lest he come and smite me, the mother with the children."

4. It was followed by a struggle with an angel lasting all night.

5. This gave rise to the phrase, " wrestling in prayer."

No. 8.

1. This prayer was offered by one of two wives who was deeply wronged.

2. The petition was that the cause of her sorrow might be removed.

3. An aged priest near by thought she was drunk.

4. Her answer led him to announce that her prayer would be granted.

5. The son who was born was one of earth's greatest men.

No. 9.

1. The greatest of all prayers for resignation to God's will.

2. It was repeated three times.

3. Bloody sweat testified to the agony of the one who prayed.

4. Three men who should have been watching were asleep.

5. The prayer was offered in a place called " The Oil Press."

No. 10.

1. The greatest prayer of intercession in the Old Testament.

2. It was offered on behalf of the Jewish people, who had committed a great sin.

3. It was offered by a man who lived so close to God that God spoke with him face to face.

4. He offered, if the people might be forgiven, himself to be blotted out of God's book of life.

5. God's answer was, "Whosoever hath sinned against me, him will I blot out of my book."

SERIES XXXII

More Bible Cities

[Read each description a line at a time, and *Go Till You Guess*. Your score for each item is the number of the line at which you obtained the answer, and the lowest total wins.]

No. 1.

1. The city whose rivers Naaman praised.
2. Abraham pursued Chedorlaomer beyond this city.
3. David captured and garrisoned the city.
4. Ahab obtained the right to establish streets of bazaars in this city.
5. The city's chief fame comes from the conversion of Saul of Tarsus.

No. 2.

1. This city was partly on an island and partly on the main land.
2. Ezekiel says of the king of this city: "Thou sealest up the sum, full of wisdom, and perfect in beauty."
3. Joel condemns this city for selling Jews into slavery to the Greeks.

4. Christ said that if his mighty works had been done in this city, it would have repented long ago.

5. Christ's visit to the neighborhood of this city was the longest journey of his ministry.

6. Paul landed at this city on the way to Jerusalem and stayed seven days, holding a prayer meeting on the beach as he left.

No. 3.

1. The city where Paul taught in the school of Tyrannus.

2. The city where Paul's teaching stirred up a riot in the theatre.

3. Paul addressed one of his most important letters to this city.

4. Timothy was placed in charge of the church there.

5. St. John is said to have been in charge there during the last years of his life.

No. 4.

1. Paul first met Aquila and Priscilla in this city.

2. His headquarters were the house of Titus Justus next to the synagogue.

3. Here Paul received a vision of Christ, encouraging him.

4. Here Gallio the proconsul refused to try Paul.

5. Paul wrote to this city two of his most important letters.

No. 5.

1. Paul sought for a long time to get to this city, but was prevented.

2. Finally he was taken there as a prisoner.

3. He wrote to it one of his greatest Epistles.

4. He sent from it letters to Philippi, Colossæ, Ephesus, and Philemon.

5. There he was finally beheaded.

No. 6.

1. Nahum called it the bloody city.

2. It was about sixty miles in circuit—three days' journey.
3. In Jonah it is called " that great city."
4. Jonah's mission there was more successful than he wished.
5. Christ said that in the judgment the men of this city would rise to condemn his generation.

No. 7.

1. A great city on the Orontes.
2. Here Christian foreign missions began.
3. Here extensive preaching of Christianity to Gentiles began.
4. Here the name " Christian " was first given.
5. From here Paul set out on his three missionary journeys.

No. 8.

1. The chief city of Cilicia.
2. It is situated on the Cydnus.
3. Its schools almost rivaled those of Athens and Alexandria.
4. Paul described it as " no mean city."
5. It was Paul's birthplace.

SERIES XXXIII

Bible Converts

[Read each description a line at a time, and *Go Till You Guess.* Your score for each item is the number of the line at which you obtained the answer, and the lowest total wins.]

No. 1.

1. He was a slave, who lived in Colossæ.
2. He ran away to Rome.
3. He was converted by Paul, who was in prison.

4. Paul sent him back to his master with a beautiful letter.
5. His name means " Profitable."

No. 2.

1. He was a very wicked king, who repented when he was made captive.
2. He sacrified his children by fire to a heathen god.
3. He killed many innocent persons, Isaiah being perhaps among them.
4. The Assyrians carried him away captive to Babylon.
5. His father was the good king, Hezekiah.

No. 3.

1. A business man of Jericho who became converted.
2. He was short of stature.
3. His business was disreputable.
4. He was won by kindness.
5. He promised complete restitution and reparation.

No. 4.

1. This convert shared in the most tragic event of history.
2. He was a robber, probably also a murderer.
3. Another, unjustly condemned, was suffering with him.
4. This sufferer won him by his evident nobility.
5. He received the promise of Paradise.

No. 5.

1. He was converted by an earthquake.
2. By that, and by the nobility of two prisoners.
3. He was in immediate danger of capital punishment, but the prisoners saved him.

4. He ministered tenderly to the prisoners.
5. He was baptized that very night.

No. 6.

1. He and the man who baptized him both had remarkable visions.
2. He was a God-fearing Gentile.
3. He lived in Cæsarea.
4. He was a Roman centurion.
5. He sent a soldier and two servants after an apostle.

No. 7.

1. He was the greatest convert ever made.
2. His conversion was a complete transformation.
3. A blinding light helped him to see the truth.
4. At once he asked Christ for orders.
5. This took place near Damascus.

SERIES XXXIV

Bible Wives

[Read each description a line at a time, and *Go Till You Guess*. Your score for each item is the number of the line at which you obtained the answer, and the lowest total wins.]

No. 1.

1. If her advice had been heeded, the most terrible of all tragedies would have been averted or postponed.
2. Some think that she was a Christian.
3. At any rate, she knew that Christ was a " righteous man."

4.   She was anxious about his fate, and had a dreadful dream about him.

5.   So she sent a warning message to her husband.

No. 2.

1.   A beautiful and noble woman with a churlish husband.

2.   By his hateful spirit her husband had aroused the resentment of a great warrior who had protected him.

3.   This warrior planned the destruction of her husband and all his house.

4.   She saved the day by herself bearing to the warrior a present and an apology.

5.   Her husband dying suddenly, she became the wife of the warrior.

No. 3.

1.   She and her husband were tentmakers.

2.   The persecution of the Emperor Claudius had driven them from Rome.

3.   Paul lived with them in Corinth.

4.   They journeyed with Paul to Ephesus.

5.   There they instructed the learned Apollos.

No. 4.

1.   The less favored of the two wives of Elkanah.

2.   She had children and the other wife had none.

3.   The wife with children continually taunted the other wife.

4.   The ugly state of affairs came to a climax during a visit to the tabernacle.

5.   God took pity on the abused wife and sent her an illustrious son.

No. 5.

1.   She was the wife of Chuza.

2. He was the steward of Herod Antipas.

3. She had been healed by Christ.

4. She attended him on his journeying and helped him with her money.

5. She was one of the women who visited the tomb early on Easter morning.

No. 6.

1. She was the Moabite ancestress of Jesus.

2. She was a widow when she followed her mother-in-law to Bethlehem.

3. For their joint support, she gleaned in a harvest field.

4. The owner of the field fell in love with her and married her.

5. Among her descendants was the great king, David.

No. 7.

1. Her name may be derived from a precious stone.

2. She and her husband were ostensibly giving to the church the price of a piece of land.

3. They sold it for more than they said they did, and kept the difference.

4. Her husband fell down dead when charged with the deceit.

5. When she came in and repeated the lie, she also fell down dead.

No. 8.

1. By a trick she was palmed off on her husband in place of her sister.

2. The husband afterwards married the sister also.

3. She was less liked than her sister, partly because of her weak eyes.

4. She had six sons and one daughter, while her sister for a long time had no children.

5.   With her husband she went to Canaan, her rival dying on the way.

No. 9.

1.   An Egyptian slave of the wife of a great patriarch.

2.   She was given to the patriarch for a wife in distrust of God's promise.

3.   Dissension arose and she was sent off into the wilderness with her son.

4.   There she would have perished if an angel had not shown her a well.

5.   Her boy's descendants were numerous, but they were wild tribes of the desert.

SERIES XXXV

Some Christians

[Read each description a line at a time, and *Go Till You Guess*. Your score for each item is the number of the line at which you obtained the answer, and the lowest total wins.]

No. 1.

1.   His name means a crown.

2.   He was one of the first deacons.

3.   He debated Christianity in the foreign-speaking synagogues of Jerusalem.

4.   He had a vision of Christ standing at the right hand of God.

5.   He was the first Christian martyr.

No. 2.

1.   His name means " manliness."

2. He was a fisher.

3. With another apostle he brought the Greeks to Jesus.

4. He brought Peter to Jesus.

5. A form of cross is named after him because he is said to have suffered martyrdom on a cross of the kind.

No. 3.

1. One of the first deacons, of the same name as one of the apostles.

2. He was a pioneer Christian preacher in Samaria.

3. He baptized Simon the sorcerer.

4. He baptized the Ethiopian treasurer.

5. He had four daughters who prophesied.

No. 4.

1. He said, " Let us also go, that we may die with him."

2. He had two names, both meaning " a twin."

3. It was to him that Christ said, " I am the way, and the truth, and the life."

4. He hailed Christ as " my Lord and my God."

5. He is best known through having missed a meeting.

No. 5.

1. Of Christ's feeling for this man the Jews said, " Behold how he loved him! "

2. The most notable words ever addressed to him were " Come forth! "

3. He was at a supper given to Christ during the week of his last passover.

4. The Jews plotted to kill him.

5. He lived with his two sisters.

No. 6.

1. Paul urged Titus to help him on a journey.
2. His teachings formed a party in the Corinthian church.
3. Paul called him " the brother."
4. He was a disciple of John the Baptist.
5. Priscilla and Aquila gave him a lesson in Christian theology.

No. 7.

1. He was uncle (or cousin) of one of the Gospel writers.
2. He sold a field and gave the proceeds to the early church.
3. He vouched for Paul to the Jerusalem Christians.
4. A heathen crowd once took him for Jupiter.
5. Once he had a sharp contention with Paul.

No. 8.

1. He was seen under a fig-tree.
2. He asked, " Can any good thing come out of Nazareth? "
3. He was an Israelite in whom was no guile.
4. He came from Cana.
5. His other name was probably Bartholomew.

No. 9.

1. Paul sent him to Corinth to correct abuses in the church there.
2. Paul took him to the first church council in Jerusalem.
3. Paul sent him to oversee the churches in Crete.
4. He afterwards went to Dalmatia.
5. Paul wrote him a letter which we have in the New Testament.

No. 10.

1. He was the first martyr among the apostles.
2. Christ called him " a son of thunder."

3.   He wanted to draw fire down from heaven on a Samaritan village.

4.   He asked for a throne next to Christ's.

5.   He was a fisherman.

No. 11.

1.   He brought Nathanael to Jesus.

2.   He was from Bethsaida.

3.   Jesus asked him, before feeding the five thousand, where they could obtain bread for the multitude.

4.   He was one of those who brought the Greeks to Jesus.

5.   He said to Jesus, " Show us the Father, and it sufficeth us."

No. 12.

1.   Christ said to him, " Get thee behind me, Satan."

2.   Christ called him a rock.

3.   Christ prayed that his faith might not fail.

4.   Christ praised his confession of him.

5.   Christ bade him feed his sheep.

SERIES XXXVI

A Group of Priests

[Read each description a line at a time, and *Go Till You Guess*. Your score for each item is the number of the line at which you obtained the answer, and the lowest total wins.]

No. 1.

1.   A man who came into prominence in the most stirring series of events in the Old Testament because he could speak well.

2. He was the father of Nadab, Abihu, Eleazar and Ithamar.
3. He helped hold up Moses' arms during a battle.
4. He made the golden calf.
5. He was the first high priest.

No. 2.

1. He was high priest when John the Baptist began his ministry.
2. Each of his five sons and also his son-in-law became high priest.
3. He was still called high priest when Christ was tried.
4. He conducted Christ's first trial.
5. He was a member of the Sanhedrin before which John and Peter were tried.

No. 3.

1. The most mysterious of all Bible priests.
2. He was " without father, without mother, without genealogy."
3. Christ was a high priest after his order.
4. He was king of Salem.
5. Abraham paid tithes to him.

No. 4.

1. He was a priest of Midian.
2. He had two names.
3. He had seven daughters.
4. One of them was Zipporah.
5. He suggested to Moses the appointment of judges.

No. 5.

1. He held it expedient that one man should die for the people.
2. He was high priest.
3. He was son-in-law of another high priest.

4. He presided over the most famous and iniquitous trial of all history.

5. He took part in the trial of Peter and John.

No. 6.

1. He bade a prophet go back to Judah.

2. He told his king that the land was not able to bear the words of this prophet.

3. The prophet foretold a terrible fate for the priest.

4. He was priest of a heathen sanctuary.

5. The prophet was Amos.

No. 7.

1. He was a priest of the course of Abijah.

2. He lived in the hill country of Judæa.

3. He was struck dumb for a time.

4. He composed the " Benedictus."

5. His son was named John.

No. 8.

1. He was a high priest of the family of Ithamar.

2. He was judge as well as priest.

3. He had two ungodly sons.

4. The ark was captured in his old age.

5. He fell off a seat and broke his neck.

No. 9.

1. He was high priest when David ate the showbread.

2. He had Zadok for associate.

3. He was the son of Ahimelech, descended from Eli.

4. He took David's part in Absalom's rebellion.

5. Solomon deposed him for siding with Adonijah.

SERIES XXXVII

More Bible Sayings

[Read each description a line at a time, and *Go Till You Guess*. Your score for each item is the number of the line at which you obtained the answer, and the lowest total wins.]

No. 1.

1. This was said by a man who prophesied, though he was no prophet.
2. It was said in response to a charge that he was prophesying for gain.
3. It was spoken in Bethel.
4. It was addressed to a priest.
5. It was spoken by a sturdy shepherd-farmer.

No. 2.

1. In this saying Christ gave a threefold account of himself.
2. It was spoken the day before his death.
3. It was said in the upper room.
4. It was spoken to Thomas.
5. It was spoken in connection with his saying, " Whither I go, ye know the way."

No. 3.

1. A saying of pride, spoken by a mighty Eastern monarch.
2. He was walking in his magnificent palace as he spoke.
3. He was thinking of the splendors of his capital.
4. His proud utterance was followed by a strange transformation.
5. Daniel had warned him of all this.

No. 4.

1. A message from Europe to Asia.
2. It was heard at night.
3. It was heard at Troas.
4. It was heard by the greatest of all missionaries.
5. It sent Christianity westward instead of eastward.

No. 5.

1. This was said when a farmer's son was unexpectedly seized with religious ecstasy.
2. He was returning from a conference with an aged religious leader, ranking next to Moses.
3. At a certain hill he was met by a band of prophets.
4. Then the young man also began to prophesy.
5. The young man afterwards became a king.

No. 6.

1. This sentence is an expression of the thorough destruction awaiting the evil.
2. It was spoken by the herald of Christ.
3. It was spoken to those whom he called " offspring of vipers."
4. It was spoken in the wilderness of Judæa.
5. It included an axe simile.

No. 7.

1. The sentence expresses the significance given to a heap of stones.
2. It was a covenant between a son-in-law and his father-in-law.
3. The first was fleeing from the second, who caught up with him.
4. The father-in-law lived in Mesopotamia.
5. The sentence is often used as a benediction.

No. 8.

1. The Lord said this to the greatest man in the Old Testament in the greatest crisis of his life.

2. An apparently insurmountable obstacle lay in his path and in the way of his people.

3. An implacable foe was in the rear.

4. They were hemmed in by mountains.

5. The great leader obeyed the command, and met with a wonderful deliverance.

No. 9.

1. A sentence from Christ's most blessed parable, describing a wasteful career.

2. The young man of whom Christ was speaking had left his father's home.

3. He was living for pleasure.

4. He was squandering his share of his father's property.

5. This sentence tells how he did it.

No. 10.

1. This was said by a great teacher, expressing the indifference and hostility of his fellow townsmen.

2. They scorned the teacher because of his lowly origin.

3. His father, and he himself, were plain working men.

4. His brothers and sisters were well known in the village.

5. Finally he was compelled to leave the village and go to live in a nearby city.

SERIES XXXVIII

Bible Writers

[Read each description a line at a time, and *Go Till You Guess*. Your score for each item is the number of the line at which you obtained the answer, and the lowest total wins.]

No. 1.

1. His name means " the gift of Jehovah."
2. His other name was Levi.
3. He lived in Capernaum.
4. He was a tax-collector.
5. He made a great feast for Jesus after his conversion.
6. He wrote one of the four Gospels.

No. 2.

1. He was " a ready scribe in the law of Moses."
2. He was also a priest.
3. He went from Babylon to Jerusalem to teach the law of God.
4. He was a leader in the first recorded Sunday school.
5. He wrote a history of his times which appears in the Bible.

No. 3.

1. He was the head of the Jerusalem church in the apostolic age.
2. He pronounced the decision of the first church council.
3. He wrote the Epistle which has been called " the Gospel of Common Sense."
4. Luther called it " an Epistle of straw " because it seemed to him to depreciate faith and exalt works.
5. He was one of the sons of Mary, our Lord's mother.

No. 4.

1. The most influential and prolific of the Old Testament writers.
2. He was historian, legislator, orator, organizer, poet, and soldier.
3. His five great Books constitute the foundation of civilization.
4. His influence on the New Testament is as profound as on the Old.
5. He was one of the few greatest men of all time.

No. 5.

1. He wrote more Books of the Bible than any other writer.
2. His Books are the standard of Christian philosophy.
3. He was the greatest man (of course omitting the God-man) of the New Testament—probably the greatest of all time.
4. His writings range from tenderness and gentle humor to the most exalted eloquence.
5. His Books—thirteen and perhaps fourteen—are all in the form of letters.

No. 6.

1. The greatest poet of the Bible and one of the greatest that ever lived.
2. His Book is for most readers the best-loved of the Old Testament.
3. It is the longest Book of the Bible.
4. It also contains the longest chapter in the Bible.
5. He did not write all of it, but his writings dominate it.

No. 7.

1. He was a doctor, and the historian of the Christian church.
2. His life of Christ has been called " the most beautiful book ever written."
3. It is notable for its Christian hymns, and for the prominence of women and angels.

4. It alone gives us the parables of the prodigal son, the good Samaritan, and the rich man and Lazarus.

5. Without his second Book we should know very little about the great life of Paul.

No. 8.

1. This Book, in one chapter, was written by one of our Lord's brothers.

2. In the first verse he speaks of a brother of his who also wrote a Book of the New Testament.

3. He exhorts his readers to "contend earnestly for the faith which was once for all delivered unto the saints."

4. He condemns certain heretics who are "clouds without water, carried along by winds."

5. He closes with a magnificent doxology.

No. 9.

1. The writer of this Book was one of Paul's helpers who displeased him by withdrawing from a dangerous journey, but in later years was restored to his favor.

2. He became a helper of Barnabas, his uncle.

3. Later he became a helper of Peter, who is said to have furnished most of the material for his Book.

4. His Book is the most vivid of the lives of Christ.

5. He had two names, one of them being John.

No. 10.

1. He wrote one thousand and five songs.

2. He spoke three thousand proverbs.

3. One of his Books is the most remarkable collection of practical wisdom ever made.

4. Another, written in his old age, is a wonderful analysis of human experience.

5. The third is an exquisite love song, probably a spiritual allegory.

No. 11.

1. He wrote a life of Christ and four other Books of the New Testament.

2. His life of Christ is marked by the profoundest spiritual insight.

3. It alone tells us about Christ's first miracle.

4. It alone relates the raising of Lazarus.

5. We owe to it the priceless discourse at the last supper and the prayer that followed.

No. 12.

1. The most brilliant of all the Bible writers, a master of exalted and magnificent prose style.

2. The seer with the surest and fullest vision of the Messiah.

3. A bit from his writings: " A man of sorrows, and acquainted with grief."

4. Another bit: " How beautiful upon the mountains are the feet of him that bringeth good tidings."

5. Another: " The people that walked in darkness have seen a great light."

SERIES XXXIX

Bible Dreams and Visions

[Read each description a line at a time, and *Go Till You Guess*. Your score for each item is the number of the line at which you obtained the answer, and the lowest total wins.]

No. 1.

1. A boy dreamed that his brothers' sheaves in the field came and bowed down before his sheaf.
2. This dream brought great trouble on the boy.
3. The dream finally came true.
4. The boy was one of the purest and noblest of all Bible characters.
5. His story has been called the most perfect story ever written.

No. 2.

1. A trial was interrupted by the message of this dream.
2. The dreamer was the wife of the judge.
3. She sent word to him, " Have thou nothing to do with that righteous man."
4. She said that she had " suffered many things in a dream because of him."
5. The message did not accomplish the desired result.

No. 3.

1. This dream was forgotten and strangely recovered.
2. It was dreamed by the most powerful monarch in the world at the time.
3. He demanded that his sages should tell him what the forgotten dream was and what it signified.

4. They could not do it, though threatened with death.

5. A young Jew, in answer to prayer, learned the dream and its interpretation.

No. 4.

1. A vision on shipboard in a great storm.

2. A vision of an angel promising that none in the ship should be lost.

3. The message came to the greatest man on board the ship, though a prisoner.

4. He announced it as coming from the God " whose I am, whom also I serve."

5. The ship was going to Rome.

No. 5.

1. The dream of a young man on his way to Haran.

2. It was a nighttime vision in a stony place.

3. The young man had a stone for a pillow.

4. It was the dream of a staircase with angels on it.

5. The young man named the place " the House of God."

No. 6.

1. A vision of a fiery cloud out of which came four living creatures.

2. Each had the face of a man, a lion, an ox, and an eagle.

3. Alongside them were wheels like beryl, and wheels within wheels.

4. Above them was a firmament of terrible crystal, and above that was a sapphire throne.

5. From the glory of the throne came a commission for a great prophet.

No. 7.

1. A vision of a great sheet let down from heaven.

2. In the sheet were many creatures, some lawful to be eaten, some unlawful.

3. The man who saw the vision was bidden to rise, kill, and eat.

4. He protested that he had never eaten anything common or unclean.

5. The answer was, "What God hath cleansed, make not thou common."

No. 8.

1. The dreamer saw God, who said, "Ask what I shall give thee."

2. The dreamer said, "I am but a little child; I know not how to go out or come in."

3. Therefore the dreamer asked for "an understanding heart."

4. This was given him, together with the riches and honor for which he did not ask.

5. The dreamer was one of the greatest of Jewish kings.

No. 9.

1. The vision of a great city falling from heaven upon the earth.

2. The wall of the city had twelve foundations, on each of them the name of an apostle.

3. The city was a perfect cube.

4. The city was of pure, transparent gold.

5. The city was lighted by God's glory.

No. 10.

1. This vision was seen in Troas.

2. It was seen by a man whose journey had been fenced in wherever he turned.

3. The vision was of a man of Europe.

4. He said, "Come over and help us."

5. This vision turned Christianity westward.

No. 11.

1. A vision seen in the year King Uzziah died.
2. A vision of the Lord sitting upon a throne, high and lifted up.
3. A vision of a live coal touching the lips.
4. A voice saying, " Whom shall I send? "
5. The prophet answering, " Here am I, send me."

No. 12.

1. A vision of the glory of God, and Jesus standing on the right hand of God.
2. A vision at the close of a trial.
3. A vision at once announced to the judges.
4. It was immediately declared to be blasphemy.
5. The name of the martyr who saw the vision means " a crown."

ANSWERS

[Throughout these answers the reference, or references, for each line will be designated by a period. Where two or more references are separated by a semicolon, they relate to the same line.]

SERIES I.—BIBLE BOOKS.

1. The Epistle of James.
2. Ecclesiastes.
3. Judges.
4. The Gospel of John.
5. Esther.
6. Deuteronomy.
7. Hebrews.
8. ¯ah.
9. The Acts.
10. Proverbs.
11. Genesis.
12. Philemon.

SERIES II.—BIBLE RIVERS AND OTHER WATERS.

1. The Jabbok. Gen. 32: 22.
2. The Jordan. Josh. 3: 17. 2 Kings 2: 8; 5: 14.
3. The Kishon. Judg. 4: 13; 5: 21. 1 Kings 18: 40.
4. The Pool of Bethesda. John 5: 2–9.
5. The Sea of Galilee, Gennesaret, or Tiberias.
6. The Pool of Siloam. Luke 13: 4. John 9: 7.
7. The Dead or Salt Sea. Ezek. 47: 6–12.
8. The Nile. Gen. 41: 17–21. Ex. 2: 5; 7: 20; 8: 3.
9. The Euphrates. Gen. 2: 14.
10. The Mediterranean. Num. 13: 29; Acts 10: 6. Ex. 23: 31. Num. 34: 6; Josh. 15: 47.
11. The Red Sea. Ex. 15: 4, 22.

SERIES III.—BIBLE SPEECHES.

1. Paul's speech on Mars' Hill. Acts. 17: 22–31.
2. Samuel's farewell address. 1 Sam. 12: 1–25.
3. Stephen before the Sanhedrin. Acts 7: 1–60.
4. Joshua's farewell addresses. Josh. 23: 1—24: 28.
5. Paul's speech from the stairs of Castle Antonia. Acts 21: 34—22: 24.
6. The Sermon on the Mount. Matt. 5, 6, 7.
7. Peter's sermon at Pentecost. Acts 2:1–41.
8. Paul's address before Agrippa. Acts 26: 1–32.
9. Moses' farewell addresses. Deuteronomy.
10. Christ's last words with the Twelve. John 14, 15, 16.

SERIES IV.—BIBLE MOTHERS.

1. The Syro-Phœnician. Matt. 15: 21–28. Mark 7: 24–30.
2. The Virgin Mary. Luke 1: 26–38. Luke 2: 51. John 2: 4. John 19: 25–27.
3. Eve. Gen. 2: 18–24. Gen. 4: 1–15. Gen. 3: 1–24.
4. Hannah, the mother of Samuel. 1 Sam. 1: 1–28. 1 Sam. 2: 18–21.
5. Eunice, mother of Timothy. 2 Tim. 1: 5; 3: 15.
6. Elisabeth, mother of John the Baptist. Mal. 4: 5, 6. Luke 1: 17. Luke 1: 39–45. Luke 3: 1–17. Mark 6: 25–28.
7. Bath-sheba, mother of Solomon. 2 Sam. 11: 1–27. 2 Sam. 12: 1–10. 2 Sam. 12: 14–23. 2 Sam. 12: 24. 1 Kings 1: 5–40.
8. The Shunammite mother. 2 Kings 4: 8–37.
9. The mother who preferred to lose her

babe rather than allow Solomon to kill it. 1 Kings 3: 16–28.
10. Peter's wife's mother. Luke 4: 38, 39. Matt. 8: 14, 15.
11. Salome, mother of James and John. Matt. 27: 56. Mark 15: 40; 16: 1. Matt. 20: 20–24.
12. Mary, the mother of John Mark. Acts 12: 12. Acts 13: 5. Acts 13: 13. Acts 15: 36–40.
13. Sarah, the mother of Isaac. Gen. 12: 5. Gen. 12: 10–20. Gen. 20: 1–7. Gen. 18: 1–10. Gen. 21: 1, 2. Gen. 22: 1–13.

SERIES V.—BIBLE BIRDS.

1. Dove. Matt. 10: 16. Luke 2: 24. Luke 3: 22. Matt. 21: 12. Gen. 8: 8–12.
2. Eagle. Ps. 103: 5. Isa. 40: 31. Prov. 23: 5. Ex. 19: 4. Matt. 24: 28.
3. Raven. Gen. 8: 7. Ps. 147: 9. Job 38: 41. Luke 12: 24. 1 Kings 17: 4–6.
4. Fowl (cock, hen). Mark 13: 35. Mark 14: 30, 68–72. Matt. 23: 37.
5. Vulture (or falcon, or kite). Deut. 14: 13, 17. Job 28: 7. Isa. 34: 15.
6. Sparrow. Ps. 102: 7. Ps. 84: 3. Matt. 10: 29.
7. Stork. Ps. 104: 17. Zech. 5: 9. Jer. 8: 7.
8. Quail. Ps. 105: 40. Ex. 16: 13. Num. 11: 31–34.
9. Ostrich. Lam. 4: 3. Job 30: 29. Job 39: 13. Isa. 13: 21. Isa. 34: 13.
10. Swallow. Ps. 84: 3. Prov. 26: 2. Isa. 38: 14. Jer. 8: 7.

SERIES VI.—BIBLE PARABLES.

1. The Prodigal Son. Luke 15: 11–32.
2. Nathan's parable of the poor man's ewe lamb. 2 Sam. 12: 1–9.
3. The Good Samaritan. Luke 10: 25–37.
4. Jotham's parable of the trees and the bramble. Judg. 9: 1–21.
5. Parable of the Sower. Matt. 13: 1–23.

6. The Two Foundations. Matt. 7: 24–27.
7. Ezekiel's vision of the deepening river. Ezek. 47: 1–12.
8. Parables of the talents and the pounds. Matt. 25: 14–30. Luke 19: 11–27.
9. Isaiah's parable of the unfruitful vineyard. Isa. 5: 1–7.
10. The Pharisee and the Publican. Luke 18: 9–14.
11. The parable of the Escaped Prisoner. 1 Kings 20: 13–43.
12. The Rich Man and Lazarus. Luke 16: 19–31.

SERIES VII.—A COMPANY OF KINGS.

1. The Pharaoh of the Exodus (Meneptah II.?). Ex. 8: 15. Ex. 6—11. Ex. 10: 20. Ex. 14: 5–9.
2. Herod Agrippa II. (with Festus and Bernice). Acts 25: 13—26: 32.
3. Ahaz. Isa. 7: 1–16. 2 Kings 16: 3, 4. 2 Kings 16: 5. 2 Kings 16: 7–9.
4. Rehoboam. 1 Kings 11: 35. 1 Kings 11: 43. 1 Kings 12: 10, 14. 1 Kings 14: 25–28.
5. Herod Agrippa I. Acts 12: 1, 2. Acts 12: 3–19. Acts 12: 20–23.
6. Jehoshaphat. 1 Kings 22: 41. 2 Kings 8: 18. 1 Kings 22: 29–33. 2 Chron. 19: 1, 2; 20: 35–37. 2 Chron. 17: 7–9.
7. Saul. 1 Sam. 10: 23. 1 Sam. 8: 10; 10: 1. 1 Sam. 9: 3. 1 Sam. 28: 7. 1 Sam. 31: 4.
8. Hiram. 1 Kings 5: 1. 1 Kings 5: 8–11; 9: 14. 1 Kings 9: 10–13.
9. Nebuchadnezzar. 2 Kings 24: 10; 25: 1–9. 2 Kings 24: 1, 20. 2 Kings 24: 15–17. Dan. 4: 28–37.

SERIES VIII.—BIBLE MOUNTAINS AND HILLS.

1. Mt. Tabor. Judg. 4: 6, 12, 14.
2. Mt. Carmel. Isa. 35: 2. 1 Kings 18: 17–46. 2 Kings 4: 25.
3. Mt. Moriah. Gen. 22: 2. Gen. 12: 6, 7. 2 Sam. 24: 18–25. 2 Chron. 3: 1.

4. Mt. Gilboa. 1 Sam. 31: 1–6. Judg. 7: 1.
5. Mt. of Olives. John 18: 1. Matt. 21: 1. Mark 11: 1. Luke 19: 29, 41. Luke 24: 50, 51.
6. Mt. Pisgah (peak, Mt. Nebo). Deut. 3: 27. Deut. 24: 6.· Josh. 12: 2, 3. Num. 23: 13, 14.
7. Mars' Hill (the Areopagus). Acts 17: 16–32.
8. Mt. Gilead. 1 Kings 17: 1. Gen. 31: 21–25. Gen. 37: 25; Jer. 8: 22.

SERIES IX.—BIBLE TREES.

1. The olive. Gen. 8: 11. Acts 1: 12.
2. The sycomore. Amos 7: 14. Luke 19: 4.
3. The palm. Ex. 15: 27. John 12: 13. Judg. 4: 5. Neh. 8: 15. Rev. 7: 9.
4. The oak (also the terebinth or turpentine tree). Gen. 35: 8. Gen. 12: 6; 13: 18. 1 Sam. 10: 3. 2 Sam. 18: 9.
5. The fig. Zech. 3: 10. Judg. 9: 10. John 1: 48. Matt. 21: 18, 19. Matt. 24: 32, 33. James 3: 12.
6. The fir. 1 Kings 5: 8. 1 Kings 6: 15. Ezek. 27: 5. 2 Sam. 6: 5. Ps. 104: 17.
7. The cedar. Isa. 2: 13. Isa. 44: 14. Ezek. 27: 5. 2 Sam. 5: 11. 1 Kings 5: 5, 6. Song 4: 11.

SERIES X.—BIBLE DAUGHTERS.

1. Miriam. Ex. 2: 4. Ex. 2: 7, 8. Ex. 15: 20, 21. Num. 12: 1–3. Num. 12: 9–15.
2. Salome. Mark 6: 17–28.
3. Jephthah's daughter. Judges 11: 29–40.
4. Rebekah. Gen. 24: 15. Gen. 24: 17–20. Gen. 24: 61–67. Gen. 25: 21–26. Gen. 27: 1—28: 5.
5. Zipporah. Ex. 2: 16–22. Ex. 18: 2–4.
6. The daughters of Philip the evangelist. Acts 21: 8–10.
7. Rachel. Gen. 29: 18, 19. Gen. 28: 10. Gen. 29: 21–26. Jer. 31: 15. Gen. 30: 22–24. Gen. 35: 16–20.

8. Achsah, daughter of Caleb. Judges 1: 11–15. Num. 13: 30.
9. Pharaoh's daughter. Ex. 2: 5–10.
10. Michal, daughter of Saul. 1 Sam. 18: 22–29. 1 Sam. 19: 11–17. 2 Sam. 6: 12–23.

SERIES XI.—BIBLE CITIES.

1. Jericho. 2 Kings 25: 5, 6. Deut. 34: 3. 2 Kings 2: 5. Josh. 2: 1. Josh. 6: 20.
2. Gilgal. Josh. 5: 7–9. Josh. 4: 19. 1 Sam. 13: 4–15. 1 Sam. 15: 12–23. 2 Sam. 19: 15, 40.
3. Hebron. Gen. 23: 2. Gen. 23: 8, 9. Judg. 1: 10–15. Josh. 15: 13–19. Josh. 20: 7.
4. Jerusalem. Josh. 15: 63. 2 Sam. 5: 6–9. 2 Kings 25: 8, 9. Ezra 2: 1, 2. Luke 19: 41.
5. Capernaum. Matt. 9: 1; Mark 2: 1. Luke 7: 1–5. Matt. 8: 5, 14. Mark 2: 1, 13, 14. Mark 2: 1–4.
6. Athens. Acts 17: 16–31.
7. Joppa. Jonah 1: 3. 2 Chron. 2: 16. Acts 9: 36–42. Acts 10: 9–16.
8. Alexandria. Acts 6: 9. Acts 18: 24, 25. Acts 27: 6. Acts 28: 11.
9. Bethel. Gen. 28: 19. Gen. 28: 17. 1 Sam. 7: 16. 1 Kings 13: 1–32. Amos 7: 10–13.
10. Babylon. Dan. 4: 28–33. Jer. 51: 37. Gen. 11: 1–9. Dan. 3: 1–7.
11. Bethlehem. Gen. 35: 16–19. Ruth 2: 1–3. 1 Sam. 16: 1. 2 Sam. 23: 15. Matt. 2: 16–18.
12. Dothan. Gen. 37: 17–28. 2 Kings 6: 8–13. 2 Kings 6: 14–17. 2 Kings 6: 18–23.

SERIES XII.—BIBLE OBJECTS.

1. Axe. 2 Kings 6: 1–7. Judg. 9: 46–49. 1 Kings 6: 7. Isa. 10: 15. Matt. 3: 10.
2. Basket. 2 Kings 10: 7. Amos 8: 1, 2. Gen. 40: 16. Acts 9: 25. Matt. 14: 20.
3. Pot. Judg. 6: 19–21. Ex. 16: 3. Ex. 16: 33. 2 Kings 4: 2, 40, 41. Eccl. 7: 6.

4. Cup. Neh. 1:11. Gen. 44:12.
   Matt. 23:25. Matt. 26:39. Ps.
   23:5.
5. Knife. Gen. 22:6. 1 Kings 18:28.
   Prov. 30:14. Prov. 23:2.
6. Table. Ex. 26:35. 2 Kings 4:10.
   Prov. 9:2. Luke 16:21. Matt.
   21:12.
7. Nail. Judg. 4:21. Isa. 22:23. Isa.
   41:7. Eccl. 12:11. John 20:25.
8. Bed. Amos 6:4. 1 Sam. 19:13.
   Mark 4:21. Mark 2:4.
9. Seed. Ex. 16:31. Ps. 126:6. Eccl.
   11:6. 1 Cor. 15:35–45. Matt.
   13:4–8, 18–23.
10. Staff. Ex. 12:11. Gen. 32:10.
    Zech. 11:7. 1 Sam. 17:40. 2 Kings
    4:29–31.
11. Shoe. Ruth 4:7, 8. Ex. 3:5. Amos
    2:6. Josh. 9:5, 13. Luke 15:22.
12. Door. Acts 12:13. Gen. 4:7. Deut.
    15:12–17. Ex. 12:7. John 10:7, 9.

SERIES XIII.—BIBLE SONGS.

1. The Christmas song at Bethlehem.
   Luke 2:13, 14.
2. Moses' song of the ark. Num. 10:35,
   36.
3. Hannah's song of thanksgiving. 1
   Sam. 2:1–10.
4. Mary's *Magnificat.* Luke 1:46–55.
5. David's lament over Saul and Jonathan. 2 Sam. 1:17–27.
6. Moses' song after the passage of the
   Red Sea. Ex. 15:1–18.
7. The *Benedictus* of Zacharias. Luke
   1:68–79.
8. The song of Deborah and Barak.
   Judg. 5.
9. The song of Moses before his death.
   Deut. 32:1–44.
10. The *Nunc dimittis* of Simeon. Luke
    2:29–32.
11. The song of Miriam. Ex. 15:20, 21.
12. The song of David when he brought
    the ark to Jerusalem. 1 Chronicles
    16:7–36.

SERIES XIV.—BIBLE BUILDINGS.

1. Solomon's palace. 1 Kings 7:1–12;
   10:18–20.

2. The tabernacle. Ex. 25:1—27:21.
3. The temple of Diana. Acts 19:35.
4. Castle or Tower of Antonia. Acts
   21:30—22:29.
5. Solomon's temple. 1 Kings 5:1—
   6:38.
6. The tower of Babel (Babylon). Gen.
   11:1–9.
7. The temple of Dagon at Gaza. Judg.
   16:23–30.
8. The second temple at Jerusalem.
   Ezra 3:6—6:15.
9. Pithom and Raamses in Egypt. Ex.
   1:8–14. Ex. 5:1–21.
10. Herod's temple at Jerusalem. Matt.
    27:51. John 2:20 does not take ac-
    count of the temple's surroundings.

SERIES XV.—BIBLE WIDOWS.

1. The widow who fed Elijah. 1 Kings
   17:8–16.
2. Anna. Luke 2:36–38.
3. The mother of Hiram. 1 Kings
   7:13, 14. 2 Chron. 2:14.
4. The widow who gave two mites.
   Mark 12:41–44.
5. The widow of Nain. Luke 7:11–17.
6. The importunate widow. Luke
   18:1–8.
7. Naomi. Ruth 1:1–22.
8. The widow whom Elisha helped. 2
   Kings 4:1–7.

SERIES XVI.—BIBLE ANIMALS.

1. Ass. Judg. 12:14. 1 Sam. 25:20.
   Num. 22:21–30. Zech. 9:9. Matt.
   21:1–6.
2. Fox. Luke 13:32. Song 2:15.
   Neh. 4:3. Judg. 15:4. Matt. 8:20.
3. Bear. Isa. 59:11. Prov. 17:12.
   Amos 5:19. 1 Sam. 17:34–36. 2
   Kings 2:23, 24.
4. Ox. Deut. 25:4. Isa. 11:7. 1 Sam.
   6:7–12. 1 Kings 19:19. Luke
   14:19.
5. Dog. 2 Kings 9:35, 36. 2 Kings
   8:13. Matt. 7:6. Matt. 15:26, 27.
   Luke 16:21.
6. Horse. Ps. 33:17. Job 39:25.

Zech. 14: 20. Ex. 15: 21. 2 Kings 9: 20.

7. Lion. Prov. 22: 13. Judg. 14: 5–20. Dan. 6: 19–24. Eccl. 9: 4. Rev. 5: 5.

8. Pig. Prov. 11: 22. Lev. 11: 7. Matt. 7: 6. Matt. 8: 28–32. Luke 15: 15.

9. Sheep. Amos 7: 15. 2 Sam. 7: 8. Luke 2: 8–11. Isa. 40: 11. John 10: 11.

10. Goat. Ex. 26: 7. Gen. 27: 9–17. Luke 15: 29, 30. Judg. 6: 19. Matt. 25: 31–33.

11. Camel. Gen. 37: 25. Gen. 24: 64. Mark 1: 6. 1 Kings 10: 2. Matt. 19: 24.

12. Wolf. Zeph. 3: 3. Isa. 11: 6. Acts 20: 29. Matt. 10: 16. Matt. 7: 15.

SERIES XVII.—BIBLE '' ALMOSTS.''

1. Joseph of Arimathæa. John 19:.38. Luke 23: 50–53. Matt. 27: 57–60. Mark 15: 42–46.

2. Gehazi. 2 Kings 4: 27. 2 Kings 4: 31. 2 Kings 5: 20–27.

3. The Rich Young Ruler. Mark 10: 17– 22. Luke 18: 18–23.

4. Felix. Acts 23: 24—24: 27.

5. Nicodemus. John 3: 1–5. John 7: 50–52. John 19: 39.

6. Balaam. Num. 22: 2—24: 25. Num. 31: 8, 16.

7. Samson. Judg. 13: 2—16: 31.

8. Ahithophel. 2 Sam. 16: 20–23. 2 Sam. 15: 12. 2 Sam. 23: 34. 2 Sam. 17: 1–23.

SERIES XVJII.—BIBLE INSECTS, ETC.

1. Ant. Prov. 30: 24, 25. Prov. 6: 6–8.
2. Hornet. Ex. 23: 28. Deut. 7: 20. Josh. 24: 12.
3. Bee. Isa. 7: 18. Ps. 118: 12. 1 Sam. 14: 43. Matt. 3: 4.
4. Moth. Job 27: 18. Isa. 50: 9. Matt. 6: 19.
5. Fly. Eccl. 10: 1. Isa. 7: 18. Ex. 18: 20–32. Matt. 12: 24.
6. Locust. Joel 2: 1–11. Matt. 3: 4. Ex. 10: 1–20.

7. Grasshopper. Num. 13: 32, 33. Isa. 40: 22. Eccl. 12: 5.
8. Spider. Prov. 30: 28. Job 8: 14. Isa. 59: 5.
9. Scorpion. Rev. 9: 1–10. Deut. 8: 15. 1 Kings 12: 11. Luke 10: 19. Luke 11: 12.

SERIES XIX.—MORE BIBLE MOUN- TAINS.

1. Mt. Hermon. Deut. 3: 8, 9. Luke 9: 28, 29. Ps. 89: 12.
2. Mt. Hor. Num. 20: 22–29. Num. 21: 4–9.
3. Mt. Zion. Ps. 50: 2. 2 Sam. 6: 12– 18. 1 Kings 8: 1–4. Ps. 2: 6; 9: 11. Ps. 48: 2.
4. Mt. Lebanon. Josh. 1: 4. 1 Kings 5: 6.
5. Sinai (Horeb). Ex. 19: 1—20: 17. Ex. 3: 1. 1 Kings 19: 8–18.
6. Ebal (on the north) and Gerizim (on the south). John 4: 20, 21. Judges 9: 7–21. Deut. 27: 9—28: 14. Josh. 8: 33–35.
7. Mt. Quarantania. Matt. 4: 1, 2.
8. Kurn Hattîn, the Horns of Hattîn, the Mount of Beatitudes. Matt. 5: 1–12.

SERIES XX.—BIBLE MIRACLES.

1. Christ raising the daughter of Jaïrus from the dead. Matt. 9: 18–31; Mark 5: 22–43; Luke 8: 40–56.
2. Elisha's making the axehead float. 2 Kings 6: 1–7.
3. Peter's healing of the lame man at the Beautiful Gate. Acts 3: 1–10.
4. Moses causing the plague of locusts in Egypt. Ex. 10: 12–20.
5. Christ's stilling of the tempest. Luke 8: 22–25.
6. The withering of the barren fig-tree. Mark 11: 12–23.
7. The fall of the walls of Jericho. Josh. 6: 1–20.
8. The healing of Malchus's ear. Luke 22: 49–51; John 18: 10, 11.
9. The blinding of Elymas. Acts 13: 6–11.

10. Water changed to wine at Cana. John 2: 1–11.
11. The increase of oil and meal. 1 Kings 17: 8–16.
12. The raising of Lazarus from the dead. John 11: 1–44.

SERIES XXI.—ANOTHER COMPANY OF KINGS.

1. David. 1 Sam. 16: 11–13. 2 Sam. 5: 6–9. 2 Sam. 7: 1–13. 1 Sam. 17: 50. Ps. 23.
2. Hezekiah. 2 Chron. 29: 1—30: 13. 2 Chron. 32: 20. 2 Kings 20: 1–11. 2 Kings 19: 20, 35, 36.
3. Belshazzar. Dan. 5: 1. Dan. 5: 2. Dan. 5: 3–28. Dan. 5: 30.
4. Herod the Great. Matt. 2: 1–22.
5. Solomon. Proverbs, Song, Ecclesiastes, Psalm 72 and 127. 1 Kings 11: 1–8. 2 Sam. 12:25.
6. Cyrus. Isa. 44: 28; 45: 1–14. Ezra 1: 1–4. Ezra 1: 5–8. Dan. 5: 30.
7. Jeroboam. 1 Kings 12: 28–30. 1 Kings 11: 26. 1 Kings 11: 28. 1 Kings 11: 29–31. 1 Kings 11: 40.
8. Asa. 2 Chron. 16: 12. 1 Kings 15: 13. 2 Chron. 14: 9–15. 1 Kings 15: 16–20. 1 Kings 15: 12.
9. Artaxerxes Longimanus. Ezra 4: 1–24. Ezra 6: 14. Ezra 7: 1–10. Neh. 2: 1, 2.
10. Zedekiah. 2 Kings 25: 7. Jer. 37: 16, 17. Jer. 38: 14. 2 Kings 25: 1–3. 2 Kings 25: 7.
11. The Pharaoh of the Oppression, probably Rameses II. Ex. 1: 8–14.
12. Ahab. 1 Kings 16: 29–33. 1 Kings 18: 17. 1 Kings 21: 1–16. 1 Kings 22: 34–37.

SERIES XXII.—BIBLE SAYINGS.

1. "Thou art the man." 2 Sam. 12: 7. Read 2 Sam. 11: 1—12: 25.
2. "I am the resurrection, and the life." John 11: 25. Read John 11: 1–44.
3. "How long go ye limping between the two sides?" Or, in the more familiar King James version, "How long halt ye between two opinions?" 1 Kings 18: 21.
4. "What must I do to be saved?" Acts 16: 30.
5. "Father, forgive them; for they know not what they do." Luke 23: 34.
6. "Am I my brother's keeper?" Gen. 4: 9.
7. "Be thou faithful unto death, and I will give thee the crown of life." Rev. 2: 10.
8. "I am doing a great work, so that I cannot come down." Neh. 6: 3.
9. "The Lord gave, and the Lord hath taken away; blessed be the name of the Lord." Job 1: 21.

SERIES XXIII.—BIBLE SOLDIERS.

1. Joshua. Num. 13: 8, 16. Ex. 17: 8–14. Num. 27: 18–23. Josh. 1: 5, 6. Josh. 11: 23.
2. Nehemiah. Neh. 2: 1. Neh. 1: 2. Neh. 2: 20. Neh. 4: 6. Neh. 6: 11.
3. Naaman. 2 Kings 5: 1–19.
4. Caleb. Num. 13: 2–30. Josh. 15: 13–19.
5. Goliath. 1 Sam. 17: 4–7, 40–49.
6. The Capernaum centurion. Matt. 8: 5-13; Luke 7: 1–10.
7. Jonathan. 1 Sam. 14: 1–15. 1 Sam. 14: 24–30, 43–45. 1 Sam. 20: 30–34. 1 Sam. 20: 42. 2 Sam. 1: 26.
8. Gideon. Judg. 7: 1. Judg. 6: 36–40. Judg. 7: 2–8. Judg. 7: 19–22.
9. Uriah. 2 Sam. 11: 1—12: 25.
10. Jephthah. Judg. 11: 1—12: 7.

SERIES XXIV.—BIBLE PROPHETS.

1. Amos. Amos 7: 14, 15. Amos 1: 1. Amos 7: 10–13.
2. Simeon. Luke 2: 25–35.
3. Elisha. 2 Kings 6: 13–17. 2 Kings 5: 1–14. 2 Kings 2: 19–22. 2 Kings 4: 38–41. 2 Kings 2: 42–44.
4. John the Baptist. Luke 1: 15. Matt. 3: 1, 2. Matt. 3: 4. Matt. 14: 3–12.
5. Jeremiah. Jer. 1: 1. Jer. 36: 20–26. Jer. 36: 4–6. Jer. 38: 6. Jer. 9: 1.
6. Agabus. Acts 11: 27, 28. Acts 21: 10, 11.

7. Joel. Joel 1, 2. Joel 2: 12–14. Joel 2: 13. Joel 2: 27.
8. Daniel. Dan. 6: 1–3. Dan. 7, etc. Dan. 8: 1. Dan. 2: 1–46. Dan. 6: 4–27.
9. Haggai. Hag. 1: 1, 2, 8. Hag. 1: 6. Hag. 2: 8.
10. Elijah. 1 Kings 19: 1–4. 1 Kings 17: 1. 1 Kings 17: 2–6. 1 Kings 18: 30–39. 2 Kings 2: 11.
11. Jonah. Jonah 1: 1–3. Jonah 1: 4— 2: 9. Jonah 1: 17. Jonah 3: 1–3. Jonah 4: 6–11.
12. Ahijah. 1 Kings 11: 29–39. 1 Kings 14: 1–18.

SERIES XXV.—BIBLE CHILDREN.

1. The little girl who served Naaman's wife. 2 Kings 5: 1–5.
2. Timothy. 1 Tim. 1: 2, 18; 2 Tim. 1: 2. 1 Tim. 4: 12. 2 Tim. 1: 5. 2 Tim. 3: 14, 15.
3. Moses. Ex. 2: 1–15.
4. The boy whose lunch was the basis of Christ's feeding of the five thousand. John 6: 1–14.
5. Solomon. 1 Kings 3: 4–15.
6. Rhoda. Acts 12: 11–19.
7. Josiah. 2 Kings 22: 1 13. 2 Kings 23: 28–30.
8. Samuel. 1 Sam. 1: 1–11. 1 Sam. 1: 21–28. 1 Sam. 3: 1–14. 1 Sam. 2: 18, 19.
9. Lads of Bethel who mocked Elisha. 2 Kings 2: 23, 24.
10. Daniel. Dan. 1: 7. Dan. 1: 8–21. Dan. 6: 1–3.
11. The Shunammite's son raised by Elisha. 2 Kings 4: 8–37.
12. David. 1 Sam. 16: 1–13.
13. Joash. 2 Kings 11: 1–20.

SERIES XXVI.—BIBLE QUEENS.

1. Jezebel. 2 Kings 9: 30. 1 Kings 18: 4. 1 Kings 19: 2, 3. 1 Kings 21: 1–14. 1 Kings 16: 31. 2 Kings 9: 35–37.
2. Esther (Hadassah). Esth. 2: 7. Esth. 9: 20–28. Esth. 2: 1–9. Esth. 5: 1, 2. Esth. 4: 16.

3. Queen of Sheba. 1 Kings 10: 1–10.
4. Athaliah. 2 Kings 11: 1–16.
5. Herodias. Matt. 14: 1–11.
6. Vashti. Esth. 1: 1–22.

SERIES XXVII.—BIBLE MEN.

1. Job. Job. 1: 1. Job 1: 12. Job 2: 10. Job 4: 7. Job 42: 10–17.
2. Obadiah. 1 Kings 18: 1–16.
3. Noah. 2 Pet. 2: 5. Gen. 6: 17–22. Gen. 6: 14, 15. Gen. 9: 20–27.
4. Obed-edom. 2 Sam. 6: 1–15.
5. Ananias. Acts 5: 1–6.
6. Isaac. Gen. 26: 22. Gen. 25: 28. Gen. 27: 1–40. Gen. 26: 12–22. Gen. 24: 1–67.
7. Malchus. John 18: 10, 11. Luke 22: 50, 51.
8. Enoch. Gen. 5: 21–24. Gen. 5: 18. Heb. 11: 5.
9. Ananias. Acts 9: 10–18.
10. Absalom. 2 Sam. 14: 25, 26. 2 Sam. 15: 4. 2 Sam. 16: 20–23. 2 Sam. 18: 9–14. 2 Sam. 18: 31–33.
11. Simon of Cyrene. Mark 15: 21. Matt. 27: 32.
12. Lot. Gen. 14: 1–16. Gen. 11: 31. Gen. 13: 1–11. Gen. 19: 1–13. Gen. 19: 23–26.

SERIES XXVIII.—BIBLE WOMEN.

1. Mary of Bethany. Luke 10: 42. Mark 14: 3; John 12: 3. Luke 10: 39. John 11: 32. John 12: 1.
2. Deborah. Judg. 4, 5.
3. Lydia. Acts 16: 11–15.
4. Jehosheba. 2 Kings 11: 1–17.
5. Phœbe. Rom. 16: 1, 2.
6. Rahab. Josh. 2: 1. Matt. 1: 5. Josh. 2: 2–7. Josh. 2: 8–11. Josh. 6: 22–25.
7. Dorcas. Acts 9: 36–42.
8. Mary Magdalene. Luke 8: 1–3. Matt. 27: 55, 56. John 20: 11–18.
9. Martha. Mark 14: 3; John 12: 2. Luke 10: 38. John 11: 21. Luke 10: 41.
10. The slave girl of Philippi. Acts 16: 16–24.

SERIES XXIX.—BIBLE FOOD AND DRINK.

1. Honey. Ezek. 3: 3. Prov. 25: 27. Ex. 16: 31. 1 Sam. 14: 24–45. Judg. 14: 5–19.
2. Butter. Ps. 55: 21. Gen. 18: 8. Judg. 5: 25. 2 Sam. 17: 29. Job 20: 17.
3. Figs. 1 Sam. 25: 18. 1 Sam. 30: 12. 2 Kings 20: 7. Neh. 13: 15. Jer. 24: 1–10.
4. Oil. Lev. 7: 11, 12. Ezek. 16: 13. Ex. 29: 2. Num. 11: 8. 2 Kings 4: 2.
5. Vinegar. Prov. 25: 20. Num. 6: 3. Ruth 2: 14. Prov. 10: 26. Matt. 27: 48.
6. Lentils. 2 Sam. 23: 11, 12. Ezek. 4: 9. 2 Sam. 17: 28. Gen. 25: 29–34.
7. Cheese. 1 Sam. 17: 18. 2 Sam. 17: 29. Job 10: 10.
8. Egg. Luke 11: 12. Isa. 59: 5. Job 6: 6.
9. Bread. Ex. 40: 22, 23. Judg. 7: 13. Luke 24: 30–35. John 6: 35. Mark 6: 35–44.
10. Milk. 1 Cor. 3: 2. 1 Pet. 2: 2. Gen. 49: 12. Judg. 5: 25. Isa. 55: 1.
11. Salt. Col. 4: 6. 2 Kings 2: 19–22. Ezra 7: 22. Matt. 5: 13. Luke 9: 50.
12. Water. Num. 20: 10–12. 1 Kings 17: 10. John 4: 7. 2 Sam. 23: 13–17. Matt. 10: 42.

SERIES XXX.—MORE BIBLE PROPHETS.

1. Hosea. Hos. 1–3. Hos. 4: 6. Hos. 4: 17. Hos. 8: 7.
2. Isaiah. Isa. 6: 6, 7. Isa. 6: 8. Isa. 1: 1. Isa. 37: 21; 38: 1, etc. Isa. 55: 6.
3. Micah. Mic. 1: 1, 14. Mic. 4: 3. Mic. 6: 8. Mic. 4: 4.
4. Ezekiel. Ezek. 5: 1–17. Ezek. 37: 1–14. Ezek. 8: 7–13. Ezek. 10: 10. Ezek. 1: 1.
5. Malachi. Mal. 3: 1. Mal. 3: 7–12. Mal. 4: 4–6. Mal. 3: 16. Mal. 3: 10.
6. Micaiah. 1 Kings 22: 1–40.
7. Zephaniah. Zeph. 1: 1. Zeph. 1: 14. Zeph. 3: 17. Zeph. 3: 5.

8. Samuel. 1 Sam. 1: 1. 1 Sam. 7: 5–14. 1 Sam. 8: 1—10: 8.
9. Zechariah. Zech. 1: 1. Zech. 13: 1.
10. Habakkuk. Hab. 2: 15. Hab. 2: 20. Hab. 2: 2. Hab. 2: 4. Hab. 3.

SERIES XXXI.—BIBLE PRAYERS.

1. Daniel's prayers. Dan. 6: 1–27.
2. Stephen's prayer. Acts 7: 60.
3. Paul's prayer in Damascus. Acts 9: 10–12.
4. Hezekiah's prayer. 2 Kings 19: 8–37.
5. Christ's prayer after the Lord's supper. John 17.
6. Solomon's prayer at the dedication of the temple. 2 Kings 8: 22–53.
7. Jacob's prayer at the Jabbok. Gen. 32: 3–32.
8. Hannah's prayer. 1 Sam. 1: 1–28.
9. Christ's prayer in Gethsemane. Luke 22: 39–46. Mark 14: 32–42.
10. Moses' prayer of intercession. Ex. 32: 30–35.

SERIES XXXII.—MORE BIBLE CITIES.

1. Damascus. 2 Kings 4: 12. Gen. 14: 15. 2 Sam. 8: 5, 6. 1 Kings 20: 34. Acts 9: 1–9.
2. Tyre. Ezek. 28: 12. Joel 3: 4–8. Matt. 11: 21. Matt. 15: 21. Acts 21: 3–6.
3. Ephesus. Acts 19: 9. 1 Tim. 1: 3.
4. Corinth. Acts 18: 1–17.
5. Rome. Rom. 1: 9–13. Acts 28: 14–16.
6. Nineveh. Nahum 3: 1. Jonah 3: 1—4: 11. Matt. 12: 41.
7. Antioch. Acts 13: 1–3. Acts 11: 19–26.
8. Tarsus. Acts 21: 39.

SERIES XXXIII.—BIBLE CONVERTS.

1. Onesimus. Philemon 8–20.
2. Manasseh. 2 Chron. 33: 1–13.
3. Zacchæus. Luke 19: 1–10.
4. The thief on the cross. Luke 23: 32, 39–43.
5. Philippian jailer. Acts 16: 19–34.
6. Cornelius. Acts 10: 1–48.
7. Paul. Acts 9: 1–9. Acts 22: 10.

SERIES XXXIV.—BIBLE WIVES.

1. Pilate's wife. Matt. 27: 19.
2. Abigail. 1 Sam. 25: 2–42.
3. Priscilla, wife of Aquila. Acts 18: 1–3. Acts 18: 18, 19. Acts 18: 24–28.
4. Peninnah. 1 Sam. 1: 1–8.
5. Joanna. Luke 8: 2, 3. Luke 24: 9–11.
6. Ruth. Matt. 1: 5. The Book of Ruth.
7. Sapphira. Acts 5: 1–11.
8. Leah. Gen. 29: 16–28. Gen. 35: 23. Gen. 35: 19; 49: 31.
9. Hagar, mother of Ishmael. Gen. 16: 3–12. Gen. 21: 8–21. Gen. 17: 20.

SERIES XXXV.—SOME CHRISTIANS.

1. Stephen. Acts 6: 5–10. Acts 7: 55–60.
2. Andrew. Mark 1: 16. John 12: 20–22. John 1: 40–42.
3. Philip the Evangelist. Acts 6: 5. Acts 8: 4–13. Acts 8: 26–40. Acts 21: 8, 9.
4. Thomas. John 11: 16. John 14: 5, 6. John 20: 28. John 20: 24–27.
5. Lazarus. John 11: 36. John 11: 43. John 12: 1, 2. John 12: 9–11. John 11: 1–3.
6. Apollos. Titus 3: 13. 1 Cor. 1: 12. 1 Cor. 16: 12. Acts 18: 24–28.
7. Barnabas. Col. 4: 10. Acts 4: 36, 37. Acts 9: 27. Acts 14: 12. Acts 15: 36–39.
8. Nathanael. John 1: 48. John 1: 46. John 1: 47. John 21: 2.
9. Titus. 2 Cor. 8: 16, 17; 12: 18. Gal. 2: 1. Titus 1: 5. 2 Tim. 4: 10.
10. James, son of Zebedee. Acts 12: 2. Mark 3: 17. Luke 9: 51–56. Mark 10: 35–41. Matt. 4: 21.
12. Philip the Apostle. John 1: 45. John 1: 44. John 6: 5–7. John 12: 20–22. John 14: 8, 9.
13. Peter. Matt. 16: 23. John 1: 42. Luke 22: 32. Matt. 16: 16–19. John 21: 15–17.

SERIES XXXVI.—A GROUP OF PRIESTS.

1. Aaron. Ex. 4: 14, 15. Ex. 6: 23. Ex. 17: 12. Ex. 32: 1–6. Ex. 28: 1.

2. Annas. Luke 3: 2. John 18: 19–24. Acts 4: 5, 6.
3. Melchizedek. Heb. 7: 3. Heb. 6: 20. Gen. 14: 17–20.
4. Jethro (Reuel). Ex. 2: 18; 3: 1. Ex. 2: 16. Ex. 2: 21. Ex. 18: 13–17.
5. Caiaphas. John 11: 49–53. John 18: 13. Matt. 26: 57–66. Acts 4: 6.
6. Amaziah. Amos 7: 10–17.
7. Zacharias. Luke 1: 5. Luke 1: 39, 40. Luke 1: 22. Luke 1: 67–79. Luke 1: 63.
8. Eli. 1 Sam. 2: 12. 1 Sam. 4: 1–18.
9. Abiathar. Mark 2: 25, 26. 2 Sam. 15: 24–29. 1 Sam. 22: 20. 2 Sam. 15: 35. 1 Kings 1: 7; 2: 26, 27.

SERIES XXXVII.—MORE BIBLE SAYINGS.

1. "I was no prophet, neither was I a prophet's son." Amos 7: 14.
2. "I am the way, and the truth, and the life." John 14: 6.
3. "Is not this great Babylon, which I have built?" Dan. 4: 30.
4. "Come over into Macedonia, and help us." Acts 16: 9.
5. "Is Saul also among the prophets?" 1 Sam. 10: 11.
6. "Even now the axe lieth at the root of the trees." Matt. 3: 10.
7. "The Lord watch between me and thee, when we are absent one from another." Gen. 31: 49.
8. "Speak unto the children of Israel, that they go forward." Ex. 14: 15.
9. "He wasted his substance with riotous living." Luke 15: 13.
10. "A prophet is not without honor, save in his own country, and in his own house." Matt. 13: 57.

SERIES XXXVIII.—BIBLE WRITERS.

1. Matthew. Matt. 9: 9. Mark 2: 14. Luke 5: 27–32.
2. Ezra. Ezra 7: 6. Ezra 7: 5. Ezra 7: 10. Neh. 8: 1–12.
3. James. Acts 15: 13. Matt. 13: 55.
4. Moses. Luke 16: 31.

5. Paul. 1 Thess. 5: 27.
6. David. Ps. 119.
7. Luke. Luke 1: 1–4. Acts 1: 1, 2.
8. Jude (Judas). Matt. 13: 55. Jude 1, 3, 12, 24, 25.
9. Mark. Acts 13: 5, 13; 15: 37–40.
10. Solomon. 1 Kings 4: 32. Proverbs. Ecclesiastes. The Song of Songs (Canticles).
11. John. John 2: 1–11. John 11: 38–44. John 14—17. 1 John 4: 15–21. Rev. 1: 1, 2.
12. Isaiah. Isa. 53: 3. Isa. 52: 7. Isa. 9: 2.

SERIES XXXIX.—BIBLE DREAMS AND VISIONS.

1. Joseph's boyhood dream. Gen. 37: 5–8.
2. The dream of Pilate's wife. Matt. 27: 19.
3. Nebuchadnezzar's dream. Dan. 2: 1–49.
4. Paul's vision on shipboard. Acts 27: 21–26.
5. Jacob's dream at Bethel. Gen. 28: 10–19.
6. Ezekiel's first vision. Ezek. 1: 1—3: 15.
7. Peter's vision at Joppa. Acts 10: 9–16.
8. Solomon's dream in Gibeon. 1 Kings 3: 4–15.
9. John's vision of the New Jerusalem. Rev. 21: 1—22: 5.
10. Paul's vision of the man of Macedonia. Acts 16: 6–10.
11. Isaiah's vision in the temple. Isa. 6: 1–13.
12. Stephen's vision of Christ. Acts 7: 54–60.